DARK PSYCHOLOGY AND MANIPULATION

How to Manipulate People, Read Body Language,

Analyze People and Stop Being Managed

- The Comprehensive Guide with Practical

Examples from Daily Life.

NATHAN S. FREEMAN

DID YOU KNOW THAT YOU CAN DOWNLOAD FOR FREE THE AUDIOBOOK VERSION OF THIS BOOK, PLUS TWO MORE?

TABLE OF CONTENTS

CHAPTER 1: WHY DARK PSYCHOLOGY AFFECTS YOU 1

CHAPTER 2: WHY DO PEOPLE LIE? 4

CHAPTER 3: THE DARK CONTINUUM 11

CHAPTER 4: 14-TRICKS (AND PHRASES) THAT MANIPULATIVE PEOPLE USE 20

CHAPTER 5: THE SUBTLE DIFFERENCE BETWEEN PERSUASION AND MANIPULATION 31

CHAPTER 6: A GLOBAL DARK EPIDEMIC? 38

CHAPTER 7: DARK PSYCHOLOGY TRIAD (NARCISSISM, MACHIAVELLIANISM, PSYCHOPATHY) 466

CHAPTER 8: HOW TOXIC PEOPLE CHOOSE THEIR FAVORITE VICTIMS 533

CHAPTER 9: METHODS OF DARK PERSUASION AND REAL-LIFE APPLICATION 599

CHAPTER 10: THE HIDDEN SIGNALS THAT PINPOINT THE BEGINNING OF CRIMINAL BEHAVIOR 688

CHAPTER 11: HOW TO SPOT AND RECOGNIZE WHEN SOMEONE IS MANIPULATING YOU IN A RELATIONSHIP AND AT WORK..........722

CHAPTER 12: METHOD OF DARK PERSUASION: HOW MANIPULATORS ACT 80

CHAPTER 13: HOW TO DEFEND YOURSELF FROM MANIPULATION AND AVOID BRAINWASHING....................................888

CHAPTER 14: HOW TO APPLY DARK PSYCHOLOGY PRACTICES IN YOUR OWN LIFE..933

CHAPTER 15: DEALING WITH AN ABUSIVE OR MANIPULATIVE PARTNER...977

CHAPTER 16: SIMPLE STRATEGIES TO READ BODY LANGUAGE EASILY 102

CHAPTER 17: 7 EASY STEPS TO TAKE CONTROL OF YOUR LIFE + 5 PRACTICES YOU CAN START APPLY RIGHT NOW 1088

BONUS CHAPTER: HOW TO ANALYZE BODY LANGUAGE (DEEPENING)..115

CONCLUSIONS...115

CHAPTER 1:

WHY DARK PSYCHOLOGY AFFECTS YOU

All of us have the possibility for killer habits as well as this potential has accessibility to our thoughts, feelings as well as understandings. As you will undoubtedly read throughout this book, all of us have this potential, but just a couple of us acts upon them. Everyone has had thoughts as well as sensations, at one time or another, of wishing to work ruthlessly. Most of us have had ideas of wanting to injure others severely without mercy. If you are truthful with your own, you will certainly have to agree you have had thoughts and also a sensation of intending to dedicate abhorrent acts.

Provided the truth, we consider ourselves a good-hearted species; one would love to think we believe these ideas, as well as feelings, would be non-existent. Unfortunately, most of us have these thoughts as well as luckily, never act on them. Dark Psychology positions some individuals that have these very same ideas, feelings, as well as assumptions, but act on them in either conscious or spontaneous means. The noticeable distinction is that they act on them while others just have fleeting thoughts and feelings of doing so.

Every one of humanity has the potential to victimize humans and even other living creatures. While numerous limits or sublimate this propensity, some act upon these impulses.

It is the study of the human problem as it connects to the emotional nature of people to prey upon others. Dark Psychology looks to understand those ideas, sensations as well as understandings that lead to human predacious actions. Dark Psychology thinks that this production is purposive and has some logical, goal-oriented inspiration 99.99% of the time. The remaining 0,01%, under Dark Psychology, is the harsh victimization of others without a purposive intent or reasonably specified by evolutionary science or religious dogma. Within the following century, predators as well as their acts of theft, violence and also misuse will come to be a global sensation and societal epidemic otherwise compressed. Religion, philosophy, psychology, and various other convictions have tried cogently to define Dark Psychology. It is true that most human behaviors, related to evil activities, is purposive and objective-oriented. There is a location where purposive behavior, as well as goal-oriented inspiration, seems to end up being ambiguous. All humankind has a storage tank of malevolent intent towards others varying from minimally meddlesome and fleeting ideas to pure psychopathic deviant habits with no cohesive rationality. This is called the Dark Continuum. Mitigating elements functioning as accelerants and attractants to approaching the Dark Selfhood, as well as where a person's criminal activities fall on the Dark Continuum, is what Dark Psychology calls Dark Aspect.

Dark Psychology is both the research study of criminal & deviant behavior as well as a conceptual framework for figuring out the possibility for evil within all people.

"Dark Psychology is not simply the dark side of our moon, yet dark side of all moons integrated."

Do you know your dark sides, how to use them and how to control them? Would you like to be able to recognize when someone is manipulating you? This book will definitely help you learn about the different nuances of dark psychology and manipulation with many real-life examples and typical phrases that manipulating people use to control you as well as your decisions. You'll increase your self-awareness and you'll be able to better manage toxic people to achieve a better life.

CHAPTER 2:

WHY DO PEOPLE LIE?

We live in a world where lying has come to be a rather usual event. Indeed, there are currently organizations focusing on truth examining political statements and also company releases to discover the constructions often provided. It's not merely political figures or business leaders with a syndicate on fibbing to us. Lies take place in a lot of residences, whether it's the little boy standing over the smashed flower holder he says he did not break, or the teen offering a tale for why she was two hours past time limit last night.

For many lies, the reasons are made complex. In several cases, it's to secure the liar from being penalized or to protect another person from penalty. The lie could also be in order to avoid being humiliated, to hide an awkward situation, or just to have others think better of the person informing the fib. Such existing isn't praiseworthy, yet not difficult to comprehend why it occurs. It's harder to fathom why some individuals usually tell lies with no apparent objective as well as when the lies are typically straightforward to disprove. Researchers stated that there are numerous reasons of why some individuals lie compulsively.

One is that the lie being told may not seem a lie to the individual saying it. Repeated liars can sometimes feel so much pressure that their memory is undependable. They attempt to eliminate that stress by claiming something that will undoubtedly make the situation work. For that specific individual, what was simply claimed is what they intend to believe. The person lying may so terribly desire the lie to be the fact that the lie becomes his or her actual truth. Individuals who repeatedly exist normally need to be in control. When the reality of a circumstance doesn't agree with such power, they generate a lie that does satisfy the story they want.

Such individuals might likewise fret they won't be respected in case the reality can leave them looking inadequately. Instead, they offer a lie that throws them in a great light, but they aren't able to see that, most of the time, what they provided has no basis in reality. It would be nice if we can think every little thing we are told, whether from that youngster with the damaged vase or from that political leader at a political rally. But that's not going to take place, and therefore it is essential for everyone to occasionally dig just a little deeper and look for the actual reality.

Pathological existing isn't a professional medical diagnosis, though it can occasionally be a sign and symptom of other problems, such as a personality disorder or a manic episode. Yet some individuals get so accustomed to lying that they do so even when there is no apparent function, and when their lies are conveniently disproven, leaving every person scratching their heads over the factor of their deceptiveness. For several years, I've dealt with a number of these people-- so-called pathological or compulsive liars-- and acquired some understanding right into the means they assume. Believe it or not, their existing makes some sense when you look at it through their eyes.

1. The lie does matter ... to them. The primary factor individuals lie is when it just doesn't issue since they do assume it matters. While everybody around them thinks it's an insignificant issue, the liar thinks it is actually critically crucial. They may be placing unjust emphasis or stress on themselves, or the problem, but you will not recognize unless you ask something like, "It appears like this problem is really important to you-- why?"

2. Levelling seems like quitting control. Usually, individuals tell lies because they are trying to manage a scenario and exert influence towards getting the choices or reactions they desire. The truth can be "inconvenient" since it might not conform to their story.

3. They do not want to disappoint you. It might not feel like it to you; however, individuals that inform lie after lie are usually anxious regarding losing the regard of those around them. They desire you to like them, be thrilled, and worth them as well as they're worried that the truth might lead you to either deny or pity them.

4. Lies snowball. I bear in mind an anime my youngsters viewed years ago regarding how lies can grow. We inform a little teeny lie, yet then to cover that lie, we need to tell an additional one, then one more, and an extra-- each gets bigger and bigger. Lastly, we're suggesting concerning the color of the skies, since to confess anything develops the potential of the whole home of cards rolling. If a persistent phoney admits to any single lie, they seem like they're confessing to being a phoney, and afterwards, you'll have a factor to mistrust them.

5. It's not a lie to them. When we are under pressure, our thinking of the big picture can be tested. Our memory of things is quite undependable: Numerous studies show that our minds are affected by lots of points, that they alter over time, which they are radically reconstructed each time we think of them. Typically, repetitive phonies feel so much stress at the moment that their memory becomes merely unstable. When they claim something, it's usually since they genuinely believe, at that moment, that it is a fact. Their mind has been overwhelmed by tension, current events, as well as their desire to find a means to make this situation work. Occasionally, this can come to be so severe that the individual virtually seems to have created a completely alternate world in their mind, one that complies with their moment-by-moment beliefs and requirements.

6. They want it to be real. Lastly, the phoney may desire their lie to be real so badly that their desire and also requires once more bewilder their impulse. "Be the adjustment you wish to see worldwide," Gandhi claimed. But sometimes, liars wish that they can make something happen by stating it over, and by believing it as hard as they ever can. In today's setting of "different realities," it's difficult not to see this as somewhat justified. One of the most important questions concerning the existing surrounds objective. It's a multifaceted topic, but scientists have broken down why people lie methodically. National Geographic put together findings regarding why individuals exist and also positioned the factors right into four major classifications.

To Promote Yourself: Simply less than 50% of lies (44%) provide the person that lies with some kind of advantage or benefit beyond defense. The person can benefit economically (16%), give the person benefits beyond money (15%), aid the person create a much better self-image (8%) or allow the person to show up amusing by making others laugh (5%).

To Secure Yourself: The various other significant factor people do it is because of for security. Only more than one-third of all lies (36%) hide some sort of error or misdeed (22%), or they aid stay clear of other individuals (14%).

To Impact Others: A tiny minority of lies (11%) affect other individuals. Myths in this category assist others (5%), hurt others (4%), or are made to be respectful or maintain social duties (2%).

Uncertain: The tiniest group of lies revolves around unpredictability (9%). Most of them are unclear to the person who lies (7%), some are considered pathological (2%). A research study in Applied Cognitive Psychology located that regular lying increases belief in a lied-about occasion and also lowers idea in real events. Lying can distort people's understanding as well as self-confidence in what's right.

Taking a look at Lies

Recognizing the nature of lies can be broken down even more by exploring their nature. For example, there are sorts of lies that disclose how something becomes a lie. On top of that, on a more useful degree, it can be helpful to see what a few of the most typical myths are in day-to-day life.

Types of Lies

How are lies created? Right here are some of the most popular sorts of lies.

Bold: Vibrant lies, or else referred to as bold-faced or barefaced lies, are apparent to people who hear the lies. These sorts of lies are so obvious that they're seen in kids more often than adults.

Deceitful: Deceptive lies are crafted meticulously and also skillfully, with the intent to misguide the individual on the obtaining end. These lies are usually subtle as well as tough to identify.

Rejection: Denial entails declining to acknowledge something that holds.

Mistake: Lies can take place by chance. People may believe that what they're claiming is right, even if that isn't the instance.

Exaggeration: Exaggerations make the incorrect assertion that something is better. For example, people may attempt to repaint an extra eye-catching picture of themselves by stating they're a lot more successful than they are. An additional example is people over-promising something to offset a blunder.

Fabrication: Manufactures purposely compose a tale or something that's not real. These types of lies often tend to be evident and can be a mark of despair.

Minimization: Reductions decrease the level of something. Typically, these kinds of lies include justification and happen when people can't reject reality. Reductions are the reverse of exaggerations.

Non-inclusion: Lies of non-inclusion omit part of the reality. For lots of people, non-inclusion is much easier to participate in than other kinds of lies because omission is easy and also doesn't involve comprising anything.

CHAPTER 3:

THE DARK CONTINUUM

The Dark Continuum is a crucial aspect to comprehend in your passage via the dark side of humanity. The Dark Continuum is defined as an imaginary conceptual line or concentric circles that all criminal, terrible, deviant, and vicious behaviors drop. The Dark Continuum includes ideas, feelings, assumptions as well as actions experienced and committed by people. The continuum varies from light to extreme and also from purposive to aimless.

Indeed, physical symptoms of Dark Psychology are up to the right of the Dark Continuum as well as extra extreme. Mental symptoms of Dark Psychology lie to the left of the continuum, yet can be similarly damaging as physical acts. The Dark Continuum is not a range of extent, in terms of variety from negative to even worse, yet specifies typologies of victimization in the ideas and actions included. When this writer also increases his thesis of the Dark Continuum, you will undoubtedly have a conceptual illustrated line depicting all kinds of Dark Psychology ranging from mild and purposive to extreme as well as pointless.

The Light Triad vs. Dark Set of three of Personality

Why are dark triad individuals so seductive? Why do they get all the research interests? Immediately his ears pricked up, and also, he asked me to send him papers on the dark triad, mentioning that he hadn't heard of the dark set of three yet that it appeared remarkable (thus proving my factor).

" I still think, in spite of everything, that people are absolutely good at heart."-- Anne Frank

When I returned to my workplace, I e-mailed some papers to David and my colleague Elizabeth Hyde. In a fast e-mail response, David just wrote back, "light set of three"? Now my ears punctured up. Was there such a thing? Had it been examined?

The dark set of three has already been well-studied. The very first one found by Delroy Paulhus and Kevin Williams in 2002, the dark background of three of individuality includes narcissism (qualified self-importance), Machiavellianism (strategic exploitation and deceit) as well as psychopathy (callousness and also resentment). While these three qualities had typically been examined primarily amongst professional populations (e.g., bad guys), Paulhus, as well as Williams, showed that each of these characteristics is plainly on a continuum-- we are all a minimum of a little arrogant, Machiavellian and crazy.

Because of their preliminary paper, a study on the topic has raised a fair bit yearly, with two-thirds of the dark set of three showing up in

2014 and 2015 alone. While each of the participants of the dark background of three has distinct attributes and associates, there is enough overlap among these "socially aversive" attributes that Paulhus has argued that they "should be examined together."

While research study on dark personalities has added to our understanding of the darker side of humanity and how each person differs in the degree to which we regularly display dark patterns of thoughts, feelings, and habits in our day-to-day lives, what about the light side of human nature?

Everyday Saints

Socially aversive individuals exist, but what about everyday saints? I'm not speaking about the person who openly does a great deal of offering and gets numerous public distinctions and awards for all of their giving (and who frequently gives to others to achieve personal success). I'm talking about the individual who radiates their light in every direction only by their being. The person who isn't continuously calculated about their offering yet sends out genuine love naturally and spontaneously since that's simply who they are.

Through many e-mail exchanges and personal conferences, David, Elizabeth and also looked at existing tests of the dark triad and also conceptualized a selection of things connecting to the contrary theoretical characteristics of each member of the dark set of three, yet we developed something that wasn't merely the reverse of the dark triad products. Our initial things related to forgiveness, count on, sincerity, caring, acceptance, seeing the most effective in individuals, and obtaining innate satisfaction from making connections with others rather than making use of people to an end.

To our shock (since we hadn't anticipated there is always has to be three variables), three distinct elements arose from our research studies, which we identified: Kantianism (dealing with individuals as ends to themselves, not mere ways), Humanism (valuing the self-respect and also worth of each person) as well as Faith in Humanity.

After several refinements of initial products (and innovative statistical evaluations carried out by Eli Tsukayama), we decided on 12 items that catch this light triad's essence.

We have now provided the Light Set of three Scale to hundreds of individuals of different ages, sexes, races, ethnic cultures, and the results are far-ranging. Initially, the light triad is not merely the opposite of the dark set of three. While the two are negatively connected, the partnership is only modest in dimension (a correlation of about.50), supporting the concept that there is at least a bit of light and dark in each of us. In my opinion, it's best to check out those that score incredibly high up on the dark set of three not as a separate variety of human (besides, to have a dark side is to be human); however, as amplified as well as unleashed variations of potentialities that exist within everybody.

With that being said claimed, it looks like Anne Frank might have been on to something in the opening quote of this article. We determined a light set of three vs. dark triad balance scores for each participant by subtracting everyone's rating on the dark background of three from their rating on the light triad. The average balance rating of the whole example was 1.3, suggesting that the ordinary person is tipped more towards the weak relative to the dark in their familiar patterns of ideas, actions as well as feelings.

Pictures of the Light and also Dark Triad.

What about regarding the different accounts of the light and also dark triad? We located that the dark triad was favorably associated with being more youthful, being male, being inspired by the power, critical sex, accomplishment as well as affiliation (however not affection), having self-enhancement values, immature defense designs, conspicuous consumption, selfishness as well as watching their imaginative work and spiritual immortality as paths to fatality transcendence. The dark triad was adversely correlated with life fulfillment, conscientiousness, agreeableness, self-transcendent values, concern, empathy, a silent ego, a belief that humans are good, and a belief that one's very own self is excellent.

The dark set of three also revealed favorable relationships with several variables that might help with one's more agentic-related objectives. For example, the dark triad was positively correlated with utilitarian moral judgment and the stamina of creativity, bravery, and leadership, as well as assertiveness, along with intentions for power, success, and self-enhancement. Additionally, an unforeseen connection between the dark triad and also curiosity was found, which was mainly local to the embracing (" I such as to do points that are a little frightening," "I choose work that are excitingly unforeseeable") as well as deprival (" It interrupts me when I do not comprehend a remedy," "It bothers me if I don't know a word") types of curiosity.

Surprisingly, after we controlled for the much more antagonistic components of the dark triad, the dark set of three showed favorable organizations with several growth-oriented results. These findings recommend that the unsympathetic and manipulative core of the dark background of three refrains from doing these individuals lots of supports. Likely, the variance left over when the malevolence-related difference of the dark triad is removed is associated with agentic extraversion (the particular facet of extraversion related to assertiveness, which might offer a safety aspect for those racking up more significant on the dark set of three).

In raw contrast, the overall image offered by the pattern of connections with the light triad was somewhat different than the dark set of three. The light set of three was connected with being older, being female, less youth changeability, in addition to greater degrees of religiosity, spirituality, complete life satisfaction, acceptance of others, a belief that is great. However, that one's self is excellent, concern, compassion, openness to experience, conscientiousness, favorable interest, having a silent vanity as well as an idea that a person can live on via nature and also sociality (having kids) after one's fatality.

People scoring more excellent on the Light Set of three Range also reported much more complete satisfaction with their relationships, skills, and freedom. They likewise reported greater levels of secure attachment style and eros in their relationships. Generally, the light triad was related to being primarily motivated by affection as well as self-transcendent worth. Many personality toughness correlated with the light set of three, including curiosity, point of view, enthusiasm, love, compassion, team effort, mercy as well as gratefulness.

Keep in mind that the taste of interest related to a light set of three-- extending (" I actively seek as much details as I can in new situations," "I check out challenging situations as a possibility to expand and also learn")-- varied from the flavor of curiosity associated with the dark triad (largely welcoming as well as deprival). Fully grown protection designs were also related to the light set of three (e.g., humor, subli- mation, altruism, expectancy), bright ideas regarding the self, the world, and one's future. Individuals racking up higher on the Light Triad Scale also reported higher self-esteem, authenticity, and a stronger feeling of self.

In general, the light/good triad does not appear to be related to any evident disadvantages, with a few possible exceptions relying on the context. The light set of three was adversely associated with the inten- tion for accomplishment and also self-enhancement (even though the light triad was positively related to productivity and also skills). Re- garding personality strengths, unlike the dark set of three, the delicate triad was uncorrelated with bravery or assertiveness. Such attributes might be essential for getting to one's more tough goals and as well as completely self-actualizing.

Additionally, according to our forecasts, the light triad was related to more generous social guilt-- consisting of survivor (" I, in some cases, feel I don't be entitled to the joy I achieved"), separation (" It makes me anxious to be far from residence for too long") and also omnipotent obligation (" I stress a lot concerning individuals I enjoy even when they seem to be great") kinds of regret. While it may be adaptive to these types of social sense of guilt for promoting relationships and re-pairing damage in a partnership, these types of responsibility may limit one's passions for worry of doing well. In contrast, others continue to be much less successful.

The light set of three was likewise associated with better "response development," which is taken into consideration by some psychother-apists as an unstable defense design (but which I conceive in my very own work as an element of fully-grown altruism). The reaction devel-opment range included the following products: "If someone mugged me as well as swiped my cash, I 'd rather be assisted than penalized" and also "I typically discover myself being extremely nice to individ-uals that by all rights I must be angry at." While having such "caring kindness" even for one's opponents is conducive to one's very own health, these mindsets, coupled with greater interpersonal shame, can make those scoring higher on the light set of three potentially much more open up to exploitation as well as emotional manipulation from those racking up higher on the dark triad. Certainly, our company believes more examination of the social communications between extreme light vs. a dark set of three markers would undoubtedly be a fascinating future research line.

Verdict.

There are restrictions on our studies and lots of areas for future research extending and developing our job. The 12-item Light Set of Three Range must be viewed as a first draft, as well as our four types of research must be seen as more exploratory than definitive.

However, we hope our research study aids stabilize the force in personality psychology. Yes, everyday psychos exist. However, so do day-to-day saints, and they are also just as worthwhile of research study attention and cultivation in a culture that sometimes neglects that not only there are benefits worldwide. Still, there are also benefits to each of us.

CHAPTER 4:

14-TRICKS (AND PHRASES) THAT MANIPULATIVE PEOPLE USE

Some individuals are truly efficient, hiding their true selves and intents. Emotional manipulators, as an example, know how to play individuals in a manner that obtains their demands fulfilled. Unfortunately, you can't always figure out you're being used until it's too late. But there are some points you can pay attention to. According to experts, there are certain lines of psychological manipulators that use all the time to control others." Emotional manipulators are people that are usually very unconfident and put quite some effort to intimidate or damage our very own healthy emotional experience," Mary Beth Somich, licensed professional therapy affiliate. They may do this by putting down others, adjusting them, or demonstrating actions that endanger the mental health and also self-worth of those around them.

Before you also reach that factor, emotional manipulators understand precisely how to make use of specific tactics in order to tempt individuals in. For example, flattery is almost always made use of. As psychotherapist as well as cognitive behavioral therapist Dr Cali Estes, informs Bustle, "They'll find as sweet, loving, alert, as well as caring almost right away. It'll feel like the excellent person has actually just walked into your life." But once they've drawn you in, their real shades will undoubtedly begin to show. So right here are some lines emotional manipulators usually use to manage others, according to specialists.

" I Told You My Tricks, It's Fair you tell Me Yours"

Affection is produced by individuals opening up, being vulnerable with each other, as well as linking. Yet when you're dealing with an emotional manipulator, that feeling of intimacy will be fake. According to Estes, as part of their "process," manipulators will typically share something about themselves that makes them look vulnerable. As an example, it might be a difficult story from childhood or something terrible that happened to them back in university. Even if it's fake, you would not be able to say so since they're very persuading.

" This is where they tell you that you are part of their 'inner circle,'" Estes states.

From there, they may ask you to share a secret about your life because you are good friends and it look fair. Once they have this info, Estes states, you are currently in their network and they can use this against you. You ought to never feel obligated to share your ideas or keys with anyone, even your companion. If any individual makes you feel inadequate, it's ALRIGHT to be dubious about their motives. If you do not want to share, you don't need to.

"This Always happens to Me"

"The common thread of all emotional manipulators stories is 'poor me'", Christine Scott-Hudson, licensed therapist and proprietor of Develop Your Life Studio, says. "Every story they say will certainly be greatly concerning what everybody else has actually done to them." If you talk to them long enough, you'll likely see that nothing is ever their mistake. According to Scott-Hudson, some may do this at an early stage as a way to develop "intimacy." A "poor me" story will make you see them as victimized, preyed on, as well as vulnerable. While it's not a poor thing to care, just take note of it. If it's a pattern, they may be manipulating you.

"I Thought You of All People Would Certainly Understand"

Psychological manipulators are competent at making others feel guilty. "If you're a compassionate individual, it may be natural or regular for you to feel others' pain and also want to care for them," Maryann W. Mathai, certified professional clinical counsellor, says. "Sadly, psychological manipulators commonly play the sufferer and exploit thoughtful caretakers who have bad (or no) borders."

If you have given them all you have got and you are not attempting to put up boundaries, they'll make you feel guilty by claiming things like, "I thought you would certainly be even more understanding," or "You said you 'd constantly be there for me but you're not." This is their way to make you questioning about yourself, when all you're trying to do is to develop a healthier dynamic. If they refuse or attempt to make you feel a lot more guilty, Mathai says the most effective point to do in this situation is to secure yourself and also leave.

"I Never Said/Did That"

"For the few who ask forgiveness, their apologies are backhanded, insincere, or criticizing." For example, if they state something hurtful in the warmth of the minute, they will not say sorry. Instead, you'll be offered an, "I'm sorry I called you that, yet you made me really mad." Not only they do not take responsibility for their very own activities, but they try to justify their wrong actions by blaming you. One of the most important things to do right here is to search for any kind of patterns. One can be forgiven. However, if they continuously refute their behavior as well as they keep blaming you, it's thought about gaslighting, which is a type of abuse.

"You're Simply Being Unreasonable"

"Toxic individuals make you feel that you are the problem when as a matter of fact you are not " Dr S. Campbell, Ph.D., psychotherapist and also couple's therapist, says. They'll try to convince you that you're illogical, incorrect or that you are the one that they need "to deal with." When somebody doubts about themselves, it's less complicated to control or manipulate them. Something you can do in this circumstance is to speak to someone close to you. Reasonably, not every little thing can be your mistake. Talking with other individuals can help you to maintain a healthy and balanced viewpoint on the circumstance so you won't be controlled.

"Are You Certain You Wished to Do That?"

The adjustment can be extremely subtle. For example, they may claim something like, "You like that show?" or "Are you sure you intend to wear that outfit?" in a way that suggests there's something incorrect with your choices.

"You can never ever see what's wrong with what you're doing, however, you feel their judgment," licensed professional psychologist, Aimee Daramus, Psy.D., says. "When you ask what's wrong with it, they may assert that you're emotional or that you're making a big deal out of it, therefore rejecting the legitimacy of your feelings."

Emotional manipulators feed off of insecurity. When you're uncertain of your own, it gives them room to offer their thoughts as well as viewpoints on what you "should" be doing. It is necessary to recognize that that judgement is a kind of disrespect.

"If you intend to keep somebody in your life, let them understand that they're welcome in your life when they will value you," Daramus states. "Refuse to be around them when they're victimizing you for their requirements, however, keep letting them understand they will be welcome in your life when they want to treat you right."

"If You Do This for Me, I'll Know You Actually Care."

"You ought to likewise look out for someone who makes declarations that drag guilt or embarrassment with them," Justin Baksh, LMHC, a primary clinical policeman of Foundations Wellness Facility. For instance, a declaration like, "If you do this, I'll know you like me," is something people make use of in order to make you feel guilty enough to do what they desire. They may utilize this as a mean to persuade you after you've currently said no. This goes back to establishing boundaries. If you now said no, they should respect that. If they keep pressing or need to consider adjustment techniques, those are significant warnings.

It isn't effortless to find when a person is attempting to manage and adjust you. So, take note of any type of patterns that elevate warnings; always trust your intestine. Psychological control can be specified as the exercise of excessive influence with mental distortion and also psychological exploitation, to confiscate power, authority, advantages or opportunities at the sufferer's expenditure.

It is essential to identify strong social impact from psychological manipulation. Substantial social implications take place in between the majority of people, and also becomes part of the give and take of valuable relationships. In mental control, someone is taking advantage of another. The manipulator purposely produces a discrepancy of power, as well as makes use of the victim to offer his or her program.

Below is a listing of fourteen "tricks" manipulative people commonly use to persuade others into a placement of drawback, with references from publications "How to Effectively Handle Manipulative Individuals" and "A Practical Guide for Manipulators to Change Towards the Higher Self". This is not indicated to be an exhaustive checklist, but rather a collection of subtle and strident examples of coercion. Not everybody that acts those ways might be deliberately trying to manipulate you. Some individuals just have deplorable practices. No matter what, it is essential to recognize these actions in circumstances where your rights, passions as well as security are in risk.

1. House Court Benefit

A manipulative individual may demand you meeting and communicate in a natural area where she or he can exercise more supremacy and control. This can be the manipulator's workplace, residence, cars and truck, or various other areas where he really feels comfortable and familiar with (and also where you lack).

2. Let You Talk First to Establish Your Baseline as well as Search for Weaknesses

Numerous salespeople do this in order to prospect you. By asking you penetrating concerns, they establish a standard about your reasoning and habits, from which they can then examine your toughness as well as weak points. This sort of questioning with a hidden agenda can likewise take place at the work place or in individual relationships.

3. Adjustment of Facts

Examples: Existing. Reason making. Two-faced. Criticizing the victim for triggering their victimization. Deformation of the fact. Strategic disclosure or withholding of crucial Information. Exaggeration. Understatement. The one-sided bias of problem.

4. Overwhelm You with Realities as well as Data

Some individuals gain "intellectual intimidation" by presuming to be the professional and most experienced on specific subjects. They overcome you by enforcing supposed truths, stats, as well as other information you might know little around. This can occur in sales and economic scenarios, in expert discussions and settlements, in addition to social and relational disagreements. By assuming experienced power over you, the manipulator hopes to better push through her or his schedule. Some individuals utilize this technique for nothing else than to feel a sense of intellectual superiority.

5. Bewilder You with Procedures and Red Tape

Specific individuals make use of administration, documentation, treatments, legislation and by-laws, committees, as well as various other obstacles, to preserve their position and power while making your life more difficult.

6. Raising Their Voice and Displaying Adverse Emotions

Some individuals elevate their voice during discussions as a form of aggressive manipulation. The presumption might be that if they raise their voice loud enough, or display unfavorable emotions, you'll submit to their threat as well as provide what they desire. This is often integrated with stable body languages such as standing or delighted gestures to raise impact.

7. Unfavorable Shocks

Some people make use of adverse surprises to put you off balance as well as get a mental advantage. This can range from reduced balling in a negotiation to an unexpected profession that they will not have the ability to come through and supply somehow. Commonly, the unanticipated unfavorable information comes without warning, so you have little time to prepare and counter their action. The manipulator may request for extra giving ins from you to proceed to work with you.

8. Giving You Little to No Time at All to Choose

This is a usual sales and arrangement tactic, where the manipulator puts pressure on you to decide before you're ready. By applying tension and control, it is hoped that you will certainly "break" and give in to the aggressor's needs.

9. Cynical Humor Created to Poke at Your Weaknesses and also Disempower You

Some manipulators like to make essential remarks, usually disguised as wit or sarcasm, to make you appear inferior and also less secure. Examples can consist of any selection of comments ranging from your appearance to your old smartphone version, from your history and qualifications to the fact that you strolled in two minutes late as well as short of breath. By making you look negative, as well as obtaining you to feel negative, the assailant hopes to impose psychological supremacy over you.

10. Always Judge as well as Criticize You to Make You Feeling Inadequate

Distinct from the previous behavior where adverse Humor is utilized as a cover, right here, by continuously marginalizing, ridiculing, and also dismissing you, she or he keeps you off-balance as well as maintains her prevalence. The assailant purposely promotes the impression that there's always something anomalous with you, and no matter how hard you try, you will always be inadequate and never be good enough. Substantially, the manipulator concentrates on the negative without giving real and positive options or using meaningful ways to aid.

11. The Silent Treatment

By intentionally not responding to your phone calls, messages, emails, the manipulator assumes power by making you wait and intends to instill doubt and uncertainty in your mind. The cold shoulder is a head game where silence is made use of as a kind of leverage.

12. Act Lack of knowledge

This is the timeless "playing foolish" tactic. By claiming she or he does not comprehend what you want, or what you want her to do, the manipulator/passive-aggressive person makes you tackle what is her responsibility, and obtains you to perspire. Some children utilize this strategy to postpone, delay and also manipulate adults right into providing for them what they don't intend to do.

13. Guilt-Baiting

Examples: Unreasonable blaming. Targeting the recipient's soft spot and holding someone responsible for the manipulator's happiness and success, or unhappiness and failures. By targeting the recipient's emotional weaknesses and vulnerability, the manipulator coerces the recipient into ceding unreasonable requests and demands.

14. Victimhood

Examples: Exaggerated or imagined personal or health issues; dependency; co-dependency. Deliberate frailty to elicit sympathy and favor. You are playing weak, powerless, or martyr. The purpose of manipulative victimhood is often to exploit the recipient's goodwill, guilty conscience, sense of duty and obligation, or protective and nurturing instinct, to obtain unreasonable benefits and concessions.

CHAPTER 5:

THE SUBTLE DIFFERENCE BETWEEN PERSUASION AND MANIPULATION

Calling somebody manipulative is an objection of that individual's character. Saying that you have been manipulated is about having been poorly treated. Adjustment is dodgy at best, and downright immoral at worst. Yet why is this? What's wrong with control? Humans affect each other all the time and in all kind of means. But what makes it unethical?

We are frequently subject to manipulation. "Gaslighting," includes encouraging somebody to question her very own judgment as well as to rely upon the manipulator's recommendations instead. Guilt trips make someone feel excessively guilty concerning falling short to do what the manipulator wants her to do.

Advertising and marketing constantly manipulate the audience by developing untrue ideas, as when we are told to think that fried chicken is a portion of natural food. Phishing as well as various other scams manipulate their victims via a combination of deceptiveness (from outright lies to spoofed contact number or Links) and playing on feelings such as greed, worry or sympathy. Then there is even more straightforward manipulation, possibly one of the most famous examples of it is when Iago adjusts Othello to develop suspicion about Desdemona's fidelity, playing on his instabilities to make him jealous with others, and working him up into a craze that leads Othello to murder his precious.

Perhaps control is wrong since it hurts the person being controlled, like manipulative cigarette advertisements contribute to disease and mortality; manipulative phishing, as well as other scams, help with identity burglary as well as various types of fraud; manipulative social strategies can support violent or unhealthy partnerships; political adjustment can provoke division and damage democracy. But the change is not always unsafe.

For example, Amy simply left an abusive yet faithful companion; however, in a weak moment point, she is tempted to get back to him. Now, imagine that Amy's good friends utilize the same methods that Iago used on Othello. They manipulate her into the wrong thinking that her ex-partner was not just violent, but also unfaithful. Even if this behavior was meant to protect Amy, she might be far better off than she would have been if her close friends didn't manipulated her. Yet, to several, it can still seem ethically dodgy. Without effort, it would undoubtedly have been morally better for her friends to use non-manipulative means to help Amy to avoid backsliding. Something remains always morally suspicious about manipulation, even when it's used to help rather than hurts the person being manipulated. So, damage cannot be the reason why manipulation is wrong.

Probably it is wrong because it involves methods to deal with other people that are naturally wrong. This idea might be specifically appealing to those influenced by Immanuel Kant's concept that principles require us to treat each other as reasonable beings as opposed to just items. Maybe the only proper method to affect the behavior of others is by logical persuasion. Therefore, any type of form of influence other than rational belief is ethically inappropriate. But this solution also falls short, for it would condemn several forms of influence that are morally benign.

For instance, much of Iago's control entails appealing to Othello's feelings. However, sob stories are not always manipulative. Ethical persuasion usually involves empathy, or efforts to communicate precisely how it would certainly really feel to have others doing to yourself what you are doing to the others. Similarly, getting somebody to fear something to feel guilty about something is genuinely immoral; or to feel a low level of self-confidence in one's actual capabilities, do not look like an adjustment. Even invites to question one's very own judgment could not be manipulative in scenarios where - possibly as a result of intoxication or strong emotions - there is an excellent factor to do so. However, not every kind of non-rational influence appears to be manipulative.

It shows up, then, that whether an influence is manipulative relies on how it is being utilized. Iago's actions are manipulative as well as wrong, since they are planned to get Othello to believe and also feel the wrong things. Iago recognizes that Othello has no reason to be envious, but he gets Othello to feel jealous anyway. This is the emotional analogue to the deception that Iago likewise practices when he sets up matters (e.g., the gone down handkerchief) to deceive Othello into believing that Iago understands are false.

By comparison, encouraging an upset good friend to stay clear of making snap judgments before cooling down is not acting manipulatively, if you recognize that your buddy's rationality is momentarily unhealthy. When a conman tries to let you feel empathy for a non-existent Nigerian royal prince, he acts manipulatively because it would be an error to feel compassion for someone that does not exist. Yet genuine interest compassion for real individuals experiencing unjust misery, is moral persuasion rather than manipulation. When an abusive companion attempts to make you feel guilty for presuming him to be unfaithful, he is acting manipulatively since he is trying to induce lost sense of guilt. However, when a buddy makes you feel a proper quantity of sense of guilt over having deserted him in his/her of need, this does not seem manipulative.

What makes an influence manipulative match with what makes it wrong: the manipulator attempts to get someone to adopt what the manipulator herself regards as an inappropriate belief, feeling or various other frames of mind. This way, manipulation look like obtainable. The manipulator might also try to get you to feel an unacceptable feeling, too much significance to the incorrect points (e.g., someone else's approval), or to doubt something (e.g., your judgment or your beloved's fidelity). The difference between control as well as non-manipulative impact depends on whether the influencer is trying to obtain a person to make some sort of error in what he believes or feels.

It is native to the human condition that we affect each other in all sorts of ways, also pure rational persuasion. Sometimes, these influences boost the other person's decision-making circumstance by leading her to think, doubt, feel or take note of the ideal things; occasionally, they weaken decision-making by leading her to believe, question, really feel or focus on the incorrect points. However, control involves purposely making use of such influences to obstruct a person's capacity to make the appropriate decision - that is the crucial immorality of manipulation.

This way of thinking of adjustment informs us something about how exactly to acknowledge it. It is tempting to believe that change is a type of influence. However, behaviors that can be used to manipulate can likewise be used non-manipulatively. If we are to recognize control, we must look not at the type of influence, but the intent of the person utilizing it. For it is the objective to break down another person's decision-making situation that is both the significance and the essential immorality of adjustment.

Change denotes persuasion with the intent to mislead, regulate or contrive the person beyond the discussion into doing something, believing something, or buying something that leaves them either damaged or without benefit.

It might also imply that you are concealing a need to manipulate them to agree with your viewpoint in such a way that will certainly profit you. And if this benefit were disclosed, that revelation would make the various other individuals far less receptive to your message because it would either:

Demonstrate a substantial prejudice in the direction of their lack of advantage in the exchange,

Demonstrate an ulterior motive for the effort at persuasion, often driven by extreme advantage, or

Some mix of both.

So, for example, let's state I was selling a vehicle to someone and I had all of my tools of persuasion as well as strategies. That individual walked into my car showroom with his family (six kids), they were seeking and also genuinely needing a family-sized, affordable car.

But then, I persuaded mom and dad that he shouldn't be acquiring a tiny van, but a two-seater convertible instead to reclaim his juvenility, and educate his kids on how essential it is to stay true to your young self, knowing well that I would have made two times the commission on that vehicle, even if it was inappropriate for them.

That's control.

Now, suppose that the very same family stated to me: "Man, I just intend to blow some cash. I should buy a six-seater, and I recognize it's totally irrational as well as I really can't afford this, however, I'm just going for the two-seater convertible"

And, what happens if, after that, I used my powerful abilities to gradually and systematically layout a conversation and a set of facts that led this parent to recognize the genuine advantage of buying a lot more cost-effective and ideal household car?

That's persuasion, not control.

I used the same set of skills to convince someone to do something that I genuinely thought was in their best interest, rather than convincing them to do something that would have profited me. In the end, persuasion approaches, devices, as well as an understanding of just how to present facts, arguments and interactions, in a way that's most likely to get someone beyond of the conversation to buy considering just your viewpoint is mere persuasion. It's the underlying intent, the web benefit as well as the honesty with which you bring this tool kit to life that creates the distinction in between persuasion and also control.

CHAPTER 6:

A GLOBAL DARK EPIDEMIC?

Humans are predators with the prospective to take advantage of others for reasons that appear to do not have any purpose and understanding.

Within the following century, predators and also their acts of theft, violence and misuse will come to be a global sensation and societal epidemic.

Sections of predators consist of cyber-stalkers, cyber-bullies, cyber-terrorist, cyber-lawbreakers, cyber-sex-related killers as well as political/religious fanatics take part in cyber warfare. Just as Dark Psychology views all criminal habits on a continuum of severity and purposive intent, the theory of iPredator conforms with the very same framework. However, involves abuse, attack as well as online victimization using Information and Communications Innovation. The interpretation of iPredator is as complies with iPredator.

iPredator

A person, team or country who, straight or indirectly, participates in exploitation, victimization, browbeating, stalking, theft or disparagement of others, using Details and Communications Technology [ICT]. Predators are driven by deviant dreams, needs for power as well as control, retribution, religious fanaticism, political reprisal, psychiatric illness, affective distortions, peer approval or personal and monetary gain. Predators can be any type of age or sex, and are not bound by financial standing, race, faith or national heritage. iPredator is a general term utilized to differentiate any person that engages in criminal, coercive, deviant or violent behaviors using ICT. Whether the transgressor is a cyber-stalker, cyber-harasser, cyber-criminal, on the internet sex-related killer, net troll, cyber-terrorist, cyber-bully, online child porn consumer/distributor, or engaged in net disparagement or dubious online deception, they drop within the range of iPredator.

The three criteria utilized to specify an iPredator include a self-awareness of causing damage to others, directly or indirectly, making use of ICT. The use of ICT to obtain, exchange as well as supply unsafe Information. Unlike human predators before the internet age, predators rely upon the wide variety of advantages provided by Internet and also Communications Modern Technology [ICT]. These supports consist of an exchange of info over far away, rapidity of info exchanged and also the excellent accessibility to data offered.

iPredators regularly trick others using ICT in the abstract and synthetic digital cosmos referred to as the 'online world'. As a result, as the internet naturally provides all ICT customers anonymity, predators layout accounts as well as diversionary tactics to stay unseen as well as untraceable. Cyberstealth, a sub-tenet of iPredator, is a hidden technique by which predators attempt to establish and also sustain full anonymity. At the same time, they participate in ICT activities preparing their next attack, investigating innovative monitoring technologies or investigating the social profiles of their next target.

Arsonist

An arsonist is a person with an obsessive fixation with fire setting. These people usually have developmental history filled with sexual as well as physical misuse. Usually, amongst serial firebugs, there is the predisposition to be loners, have few peers, and are absolutely amazed by fire and fire setting. Serial pyromaniacs are highly ritualistic and tend to display patterned actions as to their methods for starting fires. As soon as their target is set ablaze, some pyromaniacs experience sex-related arousal and wage self-pleasure while enjoying. Despite their pathological and also ritualistic patterns, the serial pyromaniac feels satisfaction in his actions.

Necrophilia

Thanatophobia, Necrophilia and Necrologies all specify the very same type of disordered person. These are individuals that have a sexual attraction for dead bodies. The Analysis and Statistical Guidebook of Mental Disorders, by the American Psychiatric Association, categorizes necrophilia as a paraphilia. A paraphilia is a biomedical term used to explain an individual's sexual arousal and obsession with objects, circumstances or people that are not alive.

Hence, a Necrophile's paraphilia is sexual stimulation by a thing, a dead individual. Experts that have assembled profiles of Necrophiles show they have remarkable trouble experiencing a capability for making love with others. For these people, intimacy or sex with the dead feels safe rather than sex-related affection with a living human. Necrophiles have revealed feeling a terrific sense of control when in the company of a body. A sense of link comes to be added to the primary demand for viewed power.

Serial Killer

A serial killer is a real human killer generally specified as a person who murders three or even more individuals over one month or less. Meetings with many serial killers have revealed they experience a cooling down duration in between each murder. The serial killer's cool off period is an affective refractory duration whereby they are briefly satisfied with their need to cause discomfort to others. Lawbreaker Psychology professionals have assumed their inspiration for killing is the quest for an experience of psychological gratification only accomplished via cruelty.

After the murder, these individuals feel a sense of liftoff incorporated with egotistical power. " 'serial killings' means a series of 3 or more killings. Sexual offence, rape, embarrassment and torture are typically included throughout the FBI training course to profile murders. Experts at the FBI have described various other inspirations in addition to rage, like looking for attention, thrill-seeking as well as financial gain. Usually, serial killers show similar patterns in their choice of targets, how they murder and methods for the body disposal. Criminal professionals learnt behavioral analysis concur serial killers have a background of considerable emotional, behavioral as well as a social pathology.

Serial killers tend to be loners that experience trouble participating connections. What is it concerning these human predators, correctly how do they function as well as mingle in their day-to-day lives? These quick profiles talk quantities concerning the dark nature of the human condition.

Along with all sharing light to severe psychopathology, they all are perceptual loners with deep-seated forces governing their decision-making capacities. The serial arsonist might not assault other people or locate satisfaction from being a human killer as does the serial killer, still, he experiences happiness and delight from his fire setup. Along with joy, he feels a sense of achievement from the destruction he has created. His episodes of fire setting are extremely risky and he can cause harm to others, yet the objective of causing bodily pain is not his modus operandi.

For the serial pyromaniac, the big reward is his sense of satisfaction as well as the altered perception of achieving a brilliant accomplishment of genius. His perverted feeling of success, sometimes, lead him to come to be sexually excited. The pyromaniac's habits are objectionable, unlawful as well as harmful, yet does not entail conscious murder. They live within a void of infernal fixation.

Although the Necrophile is not creating pain to one more individual or victimizing others, his activities are very unusual and also missing any kind of feeling of logic. The Necrophile's demand for viewed control is so dangerous that he establishes a sexual attraction for dead body. He is sexually aroused by a drab body that is expressionless and absent of warmth. Many people desire to link throughout sexual intimacy, however, Necrophile does not need this. He becomes excited by the experience of an overall and also totals detach.

The serial killer is the most despotic personalities that materialize from the dark side. In films, lawsuit as well as news protection, the serial killer is often a subject of intrigue. As an alcoholic craves his next beverage or an opiate addict wishes for his next fix, the killer becomes addicted to murder. The serial killer speaks of the satisfaction as well as a raised feeling of release as soon as his murder has happened. Unlike the Necrophile or serial firebug, the serial killer's soul undertaking is to snuff out life.

The extent to which humans will undoubtedly go for sexual gratification, regarded control or economic gain is rather considerable and also elaborate. Before the arrival of clinical improvements and the capability of society to describe deviant human behavior, beasts and demons were the root cause of such mayhem. Incapable of understanding how individuals could dedicate such wrongs behavior, esoteric beings were the only logical explanation.

Although modern culture considers itself as advanced in its capability to understand the potential for people to dedicate violent and also heinous acts, finding out just how to minimize and prevent unusual and even dangerous actions perpetrated by people, continues to be elusive. Our species is the only one that take part in actions antithetical to our survival.

"A psychopath is emotionally flat, does not have empathy for the sensations of others as well as is devoid of sorrow. Psychotics behave as if the world is to be used for their benefit, as well as they utilize deception as well as feigned feeling to manipulate others."

DID YOU KNOW THAT CAN DOWNLOAD THE AUDIOBOOK VERSION OF THIS BOOK, PLUS TWO MORE, FOR FREE?

CLICK HERE FOR AUDIBLE US

CLICK HERE FOR AUDIBLE UK

CLICK HERE FOR AUDIBLE FR

CLICK HERE FOR AUDIBLE DE

CHAPTER 7:

DARK PSYCHOLOGY TRIAD (NARCISSISM, MACHIA-VELLIANISM, PSYCHOPATHY)

Think about the Dark triad, vanity, psychopathy, as well as Machia-vellianism as the Bermuda Triangle. The traits of all three typically overlap and also develop personality accounts that are destructive and toxic, especially when it concerns intimate connections where we drop our guard down.

One female was the subject of identity fraud. Her checking account, as well as a bank card, were jeopardized. At the time, she was in love with her sweetheart, who lived with her in her house. She was speaking consistently with the FBI and suffered extreme anxiousness and emotional tension. The authorities were unsuccessful in discovering the criminal.

Her fiancé was very helpful in helping to try to find him. He comforted her, periodically bought her gifts and also took care of paying her monthly rent. When ultimately the property manager confronted her about months of fraud, she understood that the crook was, in reality, her very own boyfriend, who had been pocketing her rent money, except to purchase her presents. Her denial made it challenging to accept the truth about his callous gaslighting.

What is the Dark Triad?

This preferred term was created in 2002 by Paulhus and Williams. Dark Triad refers to three abnormally negative personality traits - vanity, psychopathy, and Machiavellianism. The latter 2 share more attributes than with narcissists. Generally, the term refers to individuals with "subclinical" signs, implying that they might not always totally have an egotistical personality disorder (NPD) or antisocial personality disorder (ASPD). Machiavellianism emerged out of Machiavelli's approach and is not a psychological health disorder.

Narcissism is identified by the quest of vanity satisfaction, a feeling of prevalence, grandiosity, dominance, and entitlement.

Machiavellianism is marked by adjustment - a determining, duplicitous, as well as amoral character, concentrated on self-involvement and personal gain.

Psychopathy is identified by callousness, impulsivity, as well as withstanding antisocial as well as vibrant habits.

Vanity: vanity comes from the Greek misconception of Narcissus, a hunter who fell in love with his representation in a pool of water, and then drowned. Narcissistic individuals can be selfish, arrogant, lacking in empathy, and oversensitive to objection.

Machiavellianism: the word comes from the famous 16th-century Italian political leader and mediator Niccolò Machiavelli. He earned prestige when his 1513 publication, "The Prince," was interpreted as a recommendation of the dark arts of cunning and deception in diplomacy. Qualities related to Machiavellianism include duplicity, manipulation, self-involvement, and an absence of both feeling and morality.

Psychopathy: characteristics connected with psychopathy include absence of empathy or sorrow, antisocial behavior, and being manipulative and unstable. It is very important to keep in mind that there is a difference between unreasonable traits and being a psychopath, generally linked criminal violence.

Typical Dark Triad Traits

A recent research study on the Dark triad has attempted to assess these three malicious individualities' differences. To different levels, all act boldly out of self-interest as well as lack compassion and regret. They're proficient at manipulation and deceive others, though their inspirations and techniques differ. They violate social standards and even ethical values and lie, cheat, rip off, take, and bully. It's believed that genetic factors underlie their personality to some degree.

Machiavellianism and psychopathy are more closely correlated due to their harmful actions, whereas narcissists are defensive and even more fragile. It is because their grandiosity and also pompousness is an appearance for much deeper sensations of inadequacy. This distinction is linked to the obvious antisocial behavior connected with psychopathy, recommending that it may be because of organic elements, such as testosterone and social standards.

All three types (vanity just to a minimal level) racked up low on agreeableness, gauged by the Big-Five-character test that examines extraversion, neuroticism, agreeableness, conscientiousness, and openness. Agreeableness varies from beauty as well as personal appeal. It involves dependability, unselfishness, straightforwardness, conformity, generosity, and discreetness, which are essential for partnerships.

Machiavellians and also psychopaths are much more lacking in conscientiousness (Why work when you can cheat and take!). Psychos have the lowest degree of neuroticism or unfavorable feelings, which makes them the most sinister. Predictably, narcissists were much more open and a lot more extroverted—visibility associates with evidence that narcissists tend to be creative.

Deception

All three characters do not have honesty and humbleness which includes sincerity, loyalty, lack of greed, and also justness. A research study of unfaithfulness revealed that all three cheat when the risk of getting caught is low. When the threat is high, psychos and Machiavellians (when their energy for reasoning is reduced) cheat anyway. Both will deliberately exist. Narcissists have high degrees of self-deception instead of deliberate dishonesty.

Psychosocial Consequences

The relative study analyzed a variety of actions, including hostility (bullying, sadism, aggressiveness, as well as violence), unpredictable way of living (impulsivity, risk-taking, and substance usage), sexual activity (bizarre fantasies, cheating, and sexual harassment), socio-emotional deficits (absence of empathy, reduced emotional intelligence), poor health (anxiety, isolation, and stress), interpersonal issues (prominence, entitlement, and self-aggrandizement), immorality (lack of values, "deadly sins," as well as ethical disengagement, i.e., "requirements don't apply to me"), and also antisocial techniques (unfaithful, existing, and even adverse wit).

Machiavellians and psychopaths scored higher in these psychosocial issues; psychopaths almost twice as high as narcissists. The highest possible ratings were among the latter one, with aggression being the highest attribute. Narcissists scored in the groups of aggressiveness, sexual problems, interpersonal troubles, and antisocial methods. Amongst all three characters, most of the top scores were because of psychopathic characteristics. When those were managed (gotten rid of), narcissism still made up interpersonal troubles.

Heartlessness

To understand the absence of empathy among the Dark Triads individualities. The research checked out sufficient understanding, which is the capacity to have suitable psychological feedback to others' emotions, cognitive empathy, and the capacity to recognize others' feelings. They discovered that all three personality types lacked affective empathy but had an unimpaired cognitive understanding. Creepily, all three felt positive checking out sad faces, and felt negative seeing happy pictures. Narcissists and also psychotics additionally felt great seeing angry faces. Psychopaths liked seeing fearful faces.

Total empathy was most affordable amongst psychopaths and Machiavellians, as well as research study found that individuals that were high on any one of the three personality profiles had the lowest active compassion. Narcissists racked up the greatest on cognitive empathy. The reality that these people are aloof to others' feelings, while keeping the ability to assess others' opinions, enables them to control people while disregarding their damage purposefully.

The Effect of Dark Triad Characteristics at Work

It's difficult to find anything positive to claim regarding the Dark Triad attributes' effect in the work environment. Someone with such an emotional makeup would display an unfavorable habit, such as being hostile, volatile, self-indulgent, and sly, or all of these combined. In his work, which he wrote in 2013, The Dark Side of Personality at the workplace, Dr. Seth Spain, an assistant teacher at Binghampton College School of Monitoring in New York city, stated that there was proof of a "relatively robust connection between Machiavellianism and also unethical decision-making in organizations."

Research Study by Delroy Paulhus and Kevin Williams, psychologists at the College of British Columbia, suggests that tendencies associated with narcissism, Machiavellianism, and psychopathy often overlap, yet the three are different entities. Further research study located the usual connections between them were dishonesty and an absence of humbleness. Research particularly looking at the Dark triad at work claims that employees with these personality qualities are "toxic". In some instances, they lead guys mainly to be much more aggressive in work environment partnerships or attempt to influence people or events extra forcefully. However, at least initially, there is proof that vanity can discover in relatively favorable, desirable methods. A narcissist will frequently make an effort with her appearance and seem to be enchanting and friendly. She may well be conscientious and also achievement-oriented - as that will certainly likewise reflect well on her. But, in time, her continuous "me, me, me" propensity might end up being enduring individuals around her.

CHAPTER 8:
HOW TOXIC PEOPLE CHOOSE THEIR FAVORITE VICTIMS

The Conversational Narcissist

Have you ever been speaking with someone that keeps interrupting you? Perhaps I should change that sentence: have you ever before been trying to talk with a person who will not let you speak a word? Conversational narcissists LOVE to speak about themselves - or simply hear themselves speaking. They do not ask you any type of questions, they do not wait your actions, and they won't stop talking. In a relationship, these individuals will undoubtedly end up being wholly self-centered and will never be attentive to your needs.

The Straitjacket

The straitjacket is somebody who wishes to manage everything and everyone around them. They intend to be in charge of what you do, what you say, and even what you think. You recognize the individual I am talking about - they freak out when you disagree with them, and will not quit, they trying to encourage you that they are right and you should do what they state. In a connection, this person will provide you with no breathing space. Beware, these people will undoubtedly go after your psychological, conversational, and mental liberty until you have nothing left. Get out while you can!

The Psychological Moocher

Likewise, a psychological moocher is known as a "spiritual vampire", because they tend to draw the positivity out of you or bleed you mentally dry. These are the people who have something depressing, harmful, or cynical to claim. In discussions and partnerships, they never see the positive and often tend to bring every person down with them. If you know someone who only have negative things to claim whenever you see them, watch out; it may not get better.

The Drama Magnet

Some toxic individuals are magnets for drama. Something is consistently wrong. Always. Almost naturally, once a problem is resolved, an additional one arises. And also, they just want your empathy, sympathy, and assistance - but not your suggestions! You provide help and even services, yet they never seem to want to deal with anything. Instead, they grumble and complain. In a partnership, drama magnets act like victims and grow in a dilemma because it makes them feel vital. Beware, you could one day become part of the dramatization.

The JJ

A JJ is a jealous-judgmental individual. Envious individuals are exceptionally hazardous because they have a lot of self-hate that they can't be happy for any individual around them. And commonly, their jealousy comes out as judgment, criticism, or chatter. According to them, everyone else is awful, tiresome, or lacking in some way. If a person starts to express jealously regarding other people, watch out, this could be a toxic individual – moreover, you never know how they talk about you behind your back.

The Fibber

I had plenty of liars in my life before. Phonies, fibbers, exaggerators. It's tiring to have a hazardous liar in your life. Whether they tell, a little lie or a significant one, it's impossible to trust a liar in a partnership. Dishonesty drains us; we regularly doubt their words. If your instinct is ringing alarm bells, then look out; go out before you lie.

The Tank

A container crushes everything in its wake. A human tank is continuously right, doesn't take any person else's sensations or concepts into account, and also consistently places themselves first. In a relationship, tanks are exceptionally arrogant as well as see their viewpoints. They usually assume they are the smartest individual in the area, so they see every conversation and individual as a challenge that has to be gained. They hardly ever see others as equates, and this can be testing when trying to form a caring connection. If you feel your concepts are being run over, or you are not being valued, get out while you still can!

8 Points that one of the most Toxic Individuals in Your Life Share

Do you know a harmful individual? Even if now you do not, eventually in your life, you're bound to have stumbled upon someone that fits the summary. Managing such an individual can be hard and drain pipes, to state the least. Indeed, it might be challenging what you could find out about yourself, and that could push you to the limits.

- **Unsafe individuals are manipulative.** Their method operandi are to obtain people to do what they desire them to do. It's all about them. They utilize other people to accomplish whatever their objective is. They forget what you want; they do not seek equality in a partnership.
- **They are judgmental.** Keep your eyes and ears open for objection: about you, what you have done, and what you didn't do. It's never about them, and they will even lie if it serves them.
- **They take no responsibility for their sensations.** Instead, their feelings are projected onto you. If you try to direct this bent on them, they will likely safeguard their perspective and take no responsibility for almost anything.
- **They do not apologize.** They don't see any reason to, since it's always another person's fault. Although they try to manage connections to serve their ends in several circumstances, they attempt to gain sympathy and focus by claiming "victim" status.
- **They are inconsistent.** It's difficult to recognize who you're with because they quite often change behavior, randomly. They might transform their viewpoints, perspectives, and actions depending on what they feel they have to accomplish or

what they wish had happened. (And they know exactly how to be kind when they desire something from you.

- **They make you prove yourself to them**. Poisonous individuals make you choose them over someone else, or something they want over something you want. Often, this becomes a "divide and overcome" dynamic in which the only choice is them, even to the point which they need you to cut off other purposeful relationships to please them.

- **They make you safeguard yourself**. They have trouble staying focused regarding particular concerns, probably since they're not thinking about your viewpoint or trying to get to an amicable verdict. Bear in mind, they are supreme manipulators: their methods might include being obscure and also approximate, in addition to draw away the attention from the focus of the discussion to exactly how you're assessing a concern - your tone, your words, and so on. They concentrate on troubles, not solutions.

- **They are not caring, encouraging, or interested in what is essential to you**. The good things that happen to you move the attention away from them and frustrate them from focusing on their objectives. Be cautious of people who gives you the fault as well as make you appear always wrong. Loyalty is not for them.

Just how to Handle Poisoning

Did anyone pop into your head while going through these toxic personality types? If you have a person in your life that you fear seeing, who doesn't respect your opinions, or that makes you feel miserable about yourself by any means, then you need just to say no to this person.

Do you feel:

- You need to save this person and also fix their troubles continuously.
- You are covering or concealing for them.
- You fear seeing them.
- You feel drained after being with them.
- You get angry, depressing, or clinically worried when you are on all sides of them.
- They gossip or are mean.
- You feel you have to impress them.
- Their drama or problems impact you.
- They overlook your requirements as well as don't hear 'no.'

You should have remarkable, encouraging, and loving individuals in your life. Life is too brief to spend time with individuals who do not assist you in being your ideal self. I hope you will utilize this short chapter as your booster shot against toxic individuals!

CHAPTER 9:

METHODS OF DARK PERSUASION AND REAL-LIFE APPLICATION

There are some persuasion strategies that a lot of successful individuals & reputable business men use. These persuasion strategies work on the subconscious and can produce first-class outcomes if properly understood and effectively used. We have researched the very best strategies out there and also summarized them for you.

Foot in the Door

Principle: This concept means that you aim to get a person agreeing to a large request by having them agree to a modest one first. By first getting consent on little things from someone, you're making this person "devoted" to help you, and so, he will do that also for bigger request, so to stay consistent with the previous decision of agreeing.

Real-life Application:

- A visitor asks you for directions. As a follow-up, they state they might get lost and also ask you to walk them there. You're most likely to agree now than if they ask the second question straight off.
- You missed class and asked your schoolmate for their notes. Consequently, you confessed to have been a tad irresponsible

this semester and requested the whole semester's notes. By first asking the little support, you raise your opportunities to obtain the huge one later - precisely, a free-ride on your classmate's notes.

- You simply fell short a crucial midterm, and the professor does not offer retakes. You choose to request comments on your work and why you fell short, adhered to by asking for a retake. You're more likely to be successful in such a scenario than asking straight for a retake.

Study:

In 1966, 2 Stanford scientists - Jonathan Freedman and Scott Fraser - chose to check the performance of FITD as a persuasion technique. They divided 156 women into four different groups. They asked the first three major groups, asking a few straightforward inquiries regarding their household kitchen items. Three days later, they asked to personally undergo their kitchen cabinet as well as brochure their products. The various other group was just approached with the second request. The first three groups had a 52.8% conformity rate, while the last group had only 22.2%.

Door in the Face

Principle: Say, would you mind running around the streets nude screaming just how awesome this write-up is? Or No? Good, could you at least share it with your pals on social media like Facebook?

The door in the face technique is the opposite of the formerly stated persuasion strategy. First, you request something huge they are not most likely to agree with, then ask something contrastingly less complicated.

Real-life Application:

- You ask a class fellow to tutor you on that particular upcoming midterm in Advanced Statistics. The schoolmate says sorry, claiming that they simply don't have the time, they've also never seen you before. Your follow-up question for their notes is, nevertheless, accepted.
- You ask your friend to lend you only 100$. After the "No," you ask, "can I get at least 20$?".
- A grocery store has a policy of requesting contributions to a charitable reason before asking the client for payment. The majority of customers would not give away, however, if the cashier asks to make a $100 donation and after that asks "just how about simply 5$," the number of gifts increases significantly.

Study:

A study was performed on whether the DITF strategy would aid with product sales. They were selling cheese to people walking past a hut in the Austrian Alps. In the initial situation, the hikers were supplied an extra pound of cheese for 4 euros.

In the 2nd circumstance, the saleswomen initially used 2 pounds of cheese for 8 euros, and also after being declined, requesting an extra pound for 4. The compliance prices are strikingly different: 9% for the first request, 24% for the 2nd.

Securing

Principle: Anchoring is a cognitive prejudice existing in many decisions process. How do you know what item is "good", as an example? You compare it to a comparable item and decide from there. This technique has a lot of different usages, one of the most-used being pricing. Anchoring, if made use of effectively, can be a powerful persuasion method.

Real-life Application:

- You're seeking to buy a brand-new vehicle, and encounter an OK offer for 10,000$. You haggle with the salesman and reduce the price to the 7,000$. You go to home satisfied & contempt, thinking how much of a deal it was. The actual worth for the automobile, however, was less than 7,000$. The initial cost of 10,000$ serves as a support, so you'll regard anything less than that as a "bargain.".
- You simply obtained a brand-new task deal, with an initial offer of 2,000$ monthly. You discuss it to 2,200$. Again, similar to the previous example, you may be obtaining low-balled. While a 10% rise over the first offer might appear appealing, it could still be less than your real worth.

Case Study:

The Economic expert used to have three various options for subscription. A) Online for 59$ B) Print for 125$ and C) Publish & Internet for 125$. On a study done on 100 MIT trainees, 16 selected alternative A and 84 picked alternative C.

Commitment & Consistency.

Principle: Individuals are prone to be constant in their actions as well as beliefs. If you make an individual commit to something small, you can make use of the initial dedication to influence them right into doing more for you.

Real-life Application:

- Most of the time, you buy from the same brands over and over. When was the last time you attempted a brand-new treat or consumed alcohol?
- " Can you help me?" "Sure." "Could you get me a beer from the store, please?" instead of, "Hey could you etc.".
- You've probably come across how the set goal can aid with efficiency. The concept is something seldom ever neglected of a self-help publication.
- Let's say you operate at an NGO as well as you're collecting cash for a particular reason. Before requesting for donations, you can ask the person whether they support the cause. If the goal is simple, they'll most absolutely respond positively. By initially asking similar questions, you're more likely to receive contributions.

Study:

Nowadays many internet websites promoting an item, utilize this principle to enroll you in their subscriber list. Their pop-ups usually check out something in the lines of, "Yes, sign me up. I love cost-free cash!" and "No, I prefer to not be successful,". While that can appear a little bit commonsensical, it does help raise conversion prices.

Social Evidence.

Principle: The majority of your friends pick this write-up for persuasion-based guidance. You should need it too. "Every person believes this, so it must be true". Social Proof is just one of the most common persuasion methods. Somebody points out a suggestion, and everyone simply can accept it - even if they all disagree with it. When making a decision, individuals consider what their peers do and think in a comparable style.

Real-life Application:

- If you have an empty idea container at your work, you may think about filling it up a bit before beginning the change. Clients are more likely to tip if they see a filled pointer jar rather than an empty one.
- You might have a higher chance to like a Facebook post if it already has many likes, rather than a post with zero.
- The reason most individuals start smoking is social proof. Therefore, everybody smokes; consequently, you must also do it - despite all the wellness worries and horrible taste.

Study:

In 1935, in an experiment carried out by Muzafer Sherif, several subjects were positioned in a dark space with a dot of light 15 feet away. They were then asked to estimate how much the dot moved. They all gave different numbers. On the 2nd day, they were grouped with each other and again asked the same question. Well, they ended agreeing on a totally different number, much from their previous one.

Authority.

Principle: * Persuasion Professionals * assume this article is the best resource of persuasion-related suggestions. Individuals appreciate authority in any field or topic, thus making yourself seem like a source of power can take you a long way.

Real-life Application:

- Most start-ups or smaller sized firms placed an "as seen on" logo design on their touchdown web pages if they've been included on significant media websites. If a company got on Techcrunch, for example, then it indicates they're kind of a big deal, as Techcrunch simply does not cover anyone.
- Item X won the most useful iOS application for 2015.
- 9/10 dental professionals believe that a particular brand of toothpaste is the best one out there. It additionally provides clean drinking water to a developing nation. As well as treatment of cancer cells.

- Agencies often tend to mention their previous customers on their landing page. This is especially accurate if they've collaborated with big business.

Case Study:

Stanley Milgram, a psychotherapist at Yale College, performed various psychological studies that later came to be known as the Milgram Experiment. This had three separates roles - the experimenter, the teacher, and the learner. The instructor, who would undoubtedly be the volunteer, would certainly ask the learner, an actor, questions. If the learner replied wrong, the teacher would administer an electric shock. The experimenter pushed the teacher to use it, even after the learner was "crying out in pain." In most cases, the teacher would just go along with the experimenter's instructions, knowing that he was causing extreme paint someone. Most teachers continued to administer the shocks even after they student stopped answering and believed he had passed out. The takeaway here is that people, at least most of them, are willing to follow an authority, even if that means acting on something that is wrong.

Scarcity.

Principle: This post expires in the next 5 secs unless you share it on Facebook. Deficiency is just one of the most-used persuasion strategies made use of by salesmen and online marketers. Individuals often tend to desire more things that are in reduced supply. If you encourage a person that something is just available for a limited time or is limited, they're more likely to desire it.

Reciprocation.

Principle: People sometimes feel obliged to return favors; despite whether the person liked the gift, they're still inclined to offer something in return. Having a person feel indebted to you will undoubtedly always be useful, raising your possibilities of getting something you want exponentially.

CHAPTER 10:

THE HIDDEN SIGNALS THAT PINPOINT THE BEGINNING OF CRIMINAL BEHAVIOR

Crime is not arbitrary; it is either intentional or unintentional. According to the theory, illegal activity occurs when the activity area of a victim or target intersects with the activity area of an offender. A person's activity area comprises daily life locations, such as house, work, college, shopping locations, amusement areas, etc. These unique places are likewise called nodes. The routes an individual take to and from these nodes are called path. Personal paths get in touch with numerous nodes developing a perimeter. This is an individual's awareness area.

Crime pattern theory states that a crime including an offender and a victim can happen only when both activity spaces cross paths. Basically, crime will happen if an area offers the opportunity for it, and it occurs within an offender's awareness space. Consequently, an area that provides shopping, recreation and restaurants, such as a shopping mall, has a higher rate of crime. This is largely due to the high number of potential victims and offenders visiting the same area and the various targets in it. It is highly probable that in such an area a lot of car theft will happen, because of all the traffic in and out of it.

Therefore, crime pattern theory gives analysts an organized way to explore patterns of behavior.

Criminals come across new opportunities for crime every day, since they move to and from personal nodes using personal paths. For example, a victim could cross an offender's awareness space when going to a new shopping center. If the shopping center has been built in an area where crime happens nearby, chances are it will exist in some if not all offender's awareness space. This theory aids law enforcement in figuring out why crime exists in certain areas. It also helps predict where crimes may happen.

Policies

- Bad guys travel on an everyday basis via a sequence of tasks. Throughout these tasks, they make decisions. When this series is repeated daily, the choices made ended up being invariable. This invariability creates an abstract guiding pattern. When decisions to commit crimes are made, this is called "crime templates."
- Usually, criminals do not work independently; they are always involved in networks such as friends or family. These bonds vary as well as typically affect the choices made by others in the same system.
- If lawbreakers make different decisions from their network, these choices and crime templates can be incorporated. The combination of these decisions helps establish crime patterns.
- Criminals or their networks commit crimes when there is a 'triggering event.' It starts a process where the criminal locates a potential target or victim that fits the crime template.

- There is a limited span within individual's daily activities. Typically, it depends upon different nodes of activity such as work, school and home, and alongside the pathways between them.
- Criminals have characteristic spatio-temporal patterns similar to that of an honest person. The most common area for a criminal to break the law is not far from their normal activity and space.
- Victims usually have passive or active locations that share boundaries with the one of the offenders. The possible victims end up being real victims once the offender's motivation to break the law is set off. The victim, anyway, should fit the offender's crime template.

Key principles

- **Awareness space:** A personal boundary formed by paths taken to and from personal nodes.
- **Personal pathway**: the way taken to and from typical locations of activity in daily life.
- **Node:** An exact location of activity regularly used, for example home, work or school.
- **Activity space:** Describes an area of activity where crime can be committed.
- **Crime generators:** A location that draws people without any premediated intention to commit a crime since the opportunity is too good to miss.
- **Crime attractors:** A attractive location for offenders because of its known prospect for crime.
- **Edges:** The limits of an individual's awareness space.
- **Critical developments:** United Kingdom police used crime pattern theory to figure out where a crime was committed and how far away from home criminals travelled to commit it. In

two years, they analyzed 258,074 crime trips and they found that most journeys were less than half a mile. Another interesting fact was that females typically travelled farther than males. This research helped the department to prevent and control crime.

CHAPTER 11:

HOW TO SPOT AND RECOGNIZE WHEN SOMEONE IS MANIPULATING YOU IN A RELATIONSHIP AND AT WORK

Have you ever had a partner who was so in your head that all of a sudden you realized you were willingly doing things you usually would never accept? If so, you have dropped victim to a master manipulator. Adjustment in a relationship is a significant issue since it's sly. Master manipulators can twist your words and activities to ensure that it appears like every mistake have ever happened was because of you. It can make you feel strange like you're not controlling your thoughts, sensations, and activities and it usually takes place before you understand it's taking place.

Manipulation has been, and still is, a massive topic of high interest. It's a weapon used by abusers and controlling partners and it's difficult to discover; it makes you look like it's your very own fault, and also, it's not simple to escape. The majority of people don't recognize they're being controlled up until it's far too late.

While you might not find it out each time (some manipulators are simply great), there are some indications that your partner is in your head. Knowing them, it can help you educate yourself to better identify when you're being manipulated.

Plain Old Bullying

This is just one of the much less subtle (and more natural to recognize) forms of control. State, for instance, your companion asks you if you intend to clean their automobile. You do not, you wish to say no. Yet the look on their face and the tone in their voice says you better clean out their auto or something bad is most likely to happen. So, your say, "I'd love to!" and afterward, you do it. This is a person using the hazard of physical violence to control you and get you to agree to do something you do not want to. Later they might say things like, "You really did not need to do that. you can have said no." This makes them appear like a hero and that it was.

What to do: This is a problematic solution since often it's more secure just to do what the manipulator desires at the time and then determine how to run away later. Some abusers will get violent to get what they want. But sometimes (non-abuse circumstances), you can begin to say your "no" . If you can't say "no" in a partnership without being afraid for your safety and security, you need to get out of it.

House Court Benefit

Control is everything about power. One of the methods utilized to gain control is to take an individual out of their environment. Believe to yourself where you live, where you hang around, whose pals you see, and where you go on dates. Are they all your partner's favored spots? Do you stay in your partner's life, yet they do not reside in yours? This could be a control strategy made to make your companion feel more in control. You're easier to control when you're not comfortable in your environments.

What to do: 50-50. You both live in each other's lives. You both only go areas where you feel comfortable. It becomes part of being in a healthy and balanced, equivalent partnership.

Yanking on Your Heart Strings

Let's say your partner finds a kitty. The non-manipulative technique would certainly be to ask you exactly how you felt about getting a kitty, going over. If you might pay for the vet care and food, figuring out how your landlord feels about cats, and establishing if it was the best option for both you and the kitten. The manipulative strategy aims to yank on your heartstrings and make you feel like an evildoer if you say no. It goes something want, "Look at his little face! He's homeless! Do you desire him to pass away cool and alone on the streets? Do you even have a heart?" There's a significant difference.

What to do: Do not let a person making the most effective choices for you, making you appear a wrong person.

If You Truly loved Me.

This's the most awful. This manipulation method asks you to show your love over and over once more by offering your partner what they desire. "If you actually loved me, you would certainly most likely go to the shop and get me some gelato!" Or perhaps, "If you truly loved me, you would certainly change your mind about having an infant." This utilizes guilt and feeling to attempt to prod or pity you right into doing something. It's a form of manipulation despite exactly how innocent it appears.

What to do: Close it down, say something like, "I can still love you with all my heart without going to get you a gelato." You can likewise request a straighter type of communication, like, "You know you can ask me to head to the store. You do not need to bet my love for you on it.

Emotional Blackmail

Psychological blackmail is ugly and unhealthy. It resembles, "I'll kill myself if you leave." Or, it can additionally appear like, "I would certainly die without you." It can be significant or informal. It's primarily a technique that utilizes anxiety, guilt, and shame to keep you under your partner's control. And do you intend to be in a connection where you're just there because someone endangered to eliminate themselves? No others' well-being or a person's life are your sole obligation.

What to do: Do not fall for it. It's a kind of manipulation and never a real threat of suicide or self-harm. Yet say "If you're feeling self-destructive, I'll call the cops or ask for aid, but I'm not going to take care of it." It appears harsh, yet it's frequently the best (and also just) thing you can do.

Playing the Target

Imagine you and your partner get in a fight. No matter who's wrong, what was said, or what dropped, your companion is just heartbroken and can't believe you would undoubtedly harm them like that, even if she is the one who created the problem. You're continually apologizing. Your companion is hurt and helpless, and looking for attention and extra love. It's a method to make you seem like a terrible, unworthy partner and to stay clear of taking responsibility for their activities.

What to do: Apologize for the feeling which you require to apologize for. Do not succumb to your partner's continuous efforts to shame you into falling on your sword. Say something like, "I am actually sorry I raised my voice, that was unnecessary. But I won't apologize for being distressed concerning what you did. Right here's how that made me feel." Plan for waterworks.

Gaslighting

Gaslighting is the form of control that make you feel like you're losing your dang mind. Your companion does consistently dubious things, like pretending they did not claim points, you did leave out info, turn the fact, re-invent the past, and assume you failed to remember fact and make you feel like you're generally losing it. When it's done long enough, you'll be like you can't trust your brain, so you must require your partner to maintain you.

What to do: Escape. Gaslighting is a significant type of abuse, plain and primary.

Convenient Neediness

When things don't go your companion's way, are they unwell or weak or looking for treatment and support? This is a kind of manipulation, even if your partner is genuinely sick. Some examples: Your companion doesn't intend to have a severe conversation with you, so they feel faint. Your companion doesn't want you to go somewhere, and unexpectedly, you cannot go either since they need you to help them with their anxiety (which is comfortably fine once you consent to stay home). Your companion cannot help you with the household chores because they have a headache or do not have the power. Your companion doesn't want you to leave them, who will take care of them? Or maybe they fake sickness so you'll feel sorry for them and also gve them more attention.

What to do: This is not a happy relationship, and you should think about leaving. But in a moment, you can make a surprise plan to take care of your partner while you go and do what you need to do. Odds are, they'll be fine.

Killing Them with Kindness

Kindness as manipulation makes you question people's motives every time they do something useful to you. A natural example of this is the typical situation where someone gives a gift to someone, or a string of thank you and the other person says, "OK, what do you like?". A more affecting type of this method is something like, "you're looking smart, I don't know why you don't attend your school session" when the real motivation is to have a partner who makes more money and get along with their happiness. Or, "I tried good things for you, it's the best that you can do" when facing things you don't want and don't like to do.

They Are Cool, Calm and Collected

When something terrible happens with women, there's conflict, or things seem to be wrong, is your partner always feel calm? This can be an experiment that makes you feel like you're showing your over-active attitude. It makes you feeling like you can't trust your emotional reactions. It's the best method your partner controls your sensitive responses. They understand and determine when something makes you nervous. Otherwise, you're just silly or dramatic, because they're super calm. They can disturb your maturity into question or mental health, and over time, you don't know or even realize you're looking to them for response when anything happens at the spot.

What to do: If you often fall for this cheating, you might need help to get back in and trust your real emotional replies. That's how affecting this manipulation can be. At the moment, the best stuff if you can do is go with your plan and remember that you don't have to express your feelings.

They're Always Joking

This is betrayed in two different. The first is where they say the words that hurt you, or blame you, but if you are getting upset, it's your fault because they were just making fun of you. It doesn't matter how bad they were; it only matters that you're sensitive and can't bear a joke. The second one it's when someone makes fun of you in front of public. If you respond negatively, you're ruining the fun or making a scene.

CHAPTER 12:

METHOD OF DARK PERSUASION:
HOW MANIPULATORS ACT

Manipulators maintain dominance with continuous, repeating, psychological manipulation, abuse, and coercive control. Typically, they're passive-aggressive. They might lie, or act caring, or pain, or be shocked by your issues - all to deflect any objection and to keep behave unacceptably. In maintaining control, manipulators tend:

- To prevent being confronted.
- To put you on the defensive.
- To make you question your own as well as your assumptions.
- To conceal their hostile intent.
- To stay clear of obligation.
- To not have to transform.

Covert Manipulative Methods

Manipulation may consist of covert aggression, such as criticism, conceited abuse, and refined forms of emotional misuse. Favored hidden weapons of manipulators are: shame, complaining, comparing, lying, rejecting, feigning lack of knowledge or innocence (e.g.," Who me !?"), blame, bribery, threatening, mind video games, assumptions, "foot-in-the-door," turnarounds, emotional blackmail, evasiveness, neglecting, inattention, phony issue, compassion, apologies, flattery, and also presents and prefers. The most typical methods are explained below:

Lying

Habitual liars do it also when it's unnecessary. They don't lie because afraid or guilty, but just to confuse you and do what they want. Some put you on the defensive with accusations and other manipulative tactics. They may also use indirect lie, like being vague or omitting things, though everything else said is true. For example, a cheater might say he or she was working late, or was at the gym, but not admit they were on an adulterous date.

Denial

This isn't unconscious denial, like not realizing you've been abused, have an addiction, or are avoiding to face the truth. This is a conscious one to deny knowledge of promises, deals, and behavior. It also includes minimization, justification and excuses. They act like if you're making a big deal over nothing to rationalize and excuse their actions, so to make you doubt about yourself or gain your sympathy.

Avoidance

Manipulators don't want to be confronted and take responsibility. They avoid conversations about their behaviors by just refusing to discuss about them. This is usually combined with an attack, like: "You're always irritating me", letting you feel blame, guilt, or shame.

Avoidance can be intelligent and imperceptible when a manipulator changes subject. It may be masked with arrogance, compliments, or something you want to hear: "You know how much I care about you." Another tactic is to be evasive and blur the facts, confuses you and let you doubt. It's easy to give someone the benefit of the doubt, getting into denial when you're hopeful about a relationship. When you have doubts, trust them!

Blame, Guilt, and Shame

These tactics involve predictions, a protection where the manipulator blames others of own behavior: "The best defense is a good offense." By shifting the blame, the manipulator stays innocent and their victims now feel guilt and shame.

Abusers typically blame anyone else. An apology is just another manipulation. Addicts typically blame their addiction on other people, their boss or spouse.

Guilt-tripping shift the focus onto you, so to weaken you while the he/she feels superior. Martyrs usually say: "After all I've done for you". Shaming makes you feel insufficient as a person, not just because of your actions.

Intimidation

Intimidation doesn't constantly involve direct threats. It can be achieved with a look or tone and declarations like: "I always find a way;" "No one's unique;" "I have powerful friends;" "You're not young anymore". Another strategy is telling a fearful story

Playing the Victim

Rather than blaming you, this "why always me" tactic arouses your guilt so that you'll do their bidding. "I don't know what to do if you don't help me out." In extreme cases they can threaten you saying they'll kill themselves if you leave. Your submission raises your resentment, damages the relationship, and encourages the manipulators to keep going with the behavior.

10 Ways Manipulators Use Emotional Knowledge for Evil.

1. They play on fear.

A manipulator will indeed overemphasize facts and exaggerate particular factors to scare you right into the action.

Technique: Be careful of statements that indicate you lack nerve or attempts to instill a concern of missing out. Make sure you have the best picture of a scenario before taking action.

2. They trick.

All of us value openness and sincerity, but manipulators hide the fact and try to show you just one side of the tale. For example, consider the supervisor or staff member who actively spreads unconfirmed reports and a chatter to acquire a tactical benefit.

Approach: Don't believe everything you listen. Instead, base your decisions on reliable resources and also ask inquiries when information isn't clear.

3. They capitalize when you enjoy it.

Commonly, we're lured into saying yes to anything when we're in a great mood or jump on opportunities that look proficient at the moment (but that we haven't analyzed). Manipulators understand precisely how to capitalize on those states of mind.

Technique: Job to increase recognition of your favorable feelings just as long as your unfavorable emotions. When it pertains to making decisions, strive to achieve equilibrium.

4. They capitalize on reciprocity.

Manipulators know it's more challenging to say no if they do something for you - so they may try to flatter, butter you up, or say yes to small favors, and after that, ask you for big ones.

Technique: Without a doubt, giving brings more happiness than receiving. Yet, it's additionally essential to understand your constraints. And also, you don't need to afraid to say no when appropriate.

5. They promote the home-court advantage.

"A manipulative person might insist on you meeting as well as connecting in a physical room where she or he can work out even more dominance as well as control", claims Preston Ni, author of Just how to Efficiently Deal with Manipulative Individuals.

These individuals may push you in a space where they feel comfortable as well as knowledgeable, like their office, residence, or any other place you might feel less comfortable.

Method: If you require to discuss, use to do so in a neutral space. If you should satisfy the individual on his/her home turf, request a beverage of water and take part in small talk upon arrival to assist you in getting your bearings.

6. They ask lots of concerns.

It's simple to talk about ourselves. Manipulators know this, and they capitalize by asking penetrating questions with prejudice - uncovering surprise weak points or details they can utilize to their advantage.

Strategy: Obviously, you shouldn't think wrong of every person that wishes to learn more about you, but beware of those who just ask concerns - while rejecting to expose the same information regarding themselves.

7. They talk swiftly.

At times, manipulators will certainly speak at a much faster pace or unique usage vocabulary and jargon in an attempt to gain an advantage.

Method: Don't be afraid to ask people to repeat or ask for more clearness. You can also duplicate their point in your words, or ask for an example - allowing you to restore the conversation.

8. They present adverse emotions.

Some people actively increase their voice or use stable body language to reveal they're discouraged and adjust your emotions. (Basketball instructors are masters at this.).

Approach: Exercise the time out. If somebody demonstrates a strong feeling, take a minute before reacting. In some instances, you might also walk away for a few minutes.

9. They provide you a minimal time to act.

An individual might try and force you to act very fast. In doing so, they intend to coerce you right into a decision before you have time to evaluate the repercussions.

Technique: Do not submit to unreasonable needs. If your partner decline to give you more time, you're far better off seeking what you need elsewhere.

10. They offer you the silent treatment.

"By purposely not replying to your telephone calls, text messages, e-mails, or other questions, the manipulator acquires power by making you wait, and also plans to place uncertainty and unpredictability in your mind," says Ni.

Strategy: After you tried with communication to a reasonable level, offer your companion a deadline. In scenarios where options are inaccessible, an honest conversation addressing his/her communication style may be required.

CHAPTER 13:

HOW TO DEFEND YOURSELF FROM MANIPULATION AND AVOID BRAINWASHING

The term "brainwashing" was first used in the 1950s by American reporter Edward Seeker, reporting on American soldiers' treatment in Chinese prison camps during the Korean Battle. Persuading techniques have been documented as far back as the Egyptian Publication of the Dead and used by violent partners and parents, self-proclaimed psychics, cult leaders, secret cultures, revolutionaries, and authoritarians to bring others under their thumbs as well as voluntarily manipulate them. These techniques don't involve exotic weapons or unique powers; however, they do need an understanding of the human mind and also a need to manipulate it. By understanding these strategies, you can better learn how to protect yourself.

Recognizing Brainwashing Strategies

Understand that those who try to brainwash others tend to prey upon the weak as well as unprotected. Not everyone is affected by mind control, but particular people are at risk more than others. A competent manipulator knows what to find and targets in people who are experiencing a challenging time in their life or an adjustment that may or might not be of their own making. Possible prospects consist of:

- People who have actually lost their work and also worry about their future.
- Just recently separated people, mainly when the separation was a bitter one.
- Those are suffering from remaining health problems, precisely one they do not understand.
- Individuals who have shed a liked one, especially if they were extremely near that person, had a few other good colleagues.
- Young people far away from home for the first time. These are particular favorites of spiritual cult leaders.
- People who are considered socially unpleasant by their peers. They frequently tend to be loners yet look for like-minded individuals.
- One particular predative strategy is to learn sufficient info about the person and his/her belief system to explain the person's misfortune in a constant manner, keeping that belief system. Later on, this can be increased to describe history as a whole with that idea system, while discreetly customizing it to the brainwasher's analysis.

Know individuals who attempt to separate you or someone you recognize from outside impacts. Individuals experiencing an individual tragedy or other significant life adjustment are inclined to feel lonely, a skilled brain-washer works to enhance those feelings of solitude. This isolation can take several forms.

- For youths in a cult, it might be preventing them from calling their family and friends.

- It may imply never allowing the sufferer out of the abuser's sight or allowing contact with family and friends
- for a better half in a violent partnership.
- It might entail separating prisoners from one another for detainees in an adversary prison camp while subjecting them to subtle or overt kinds of torture.

Expect strikes on the target's self-worth. The target needs to be broken down, so the brainwasher can reconstruct the victim in his or her image. This can be done with both psychological and physical methods, long enough to physically and psychologically wear down the target.

- Psychological tortures may start with lying to the victim and then proceed to humiliating or frightening the sufferer. This kind of torment can be finished with words or gestures, ranging from an expression of displeasure to getting into the victim's personal space.
- Psychological tortures are not nice, naturally, yet might start with spoken disrespects, and then progress to badgering, spitting, or much more dehumanizing things such as stripping the victim to be photographed or simply looked at.
- Physical tortures may include malnourishment, cold, rest depriving, whippings, mutilations, and others; none serve society. Physical pain is typically utilized by abusive moms and dads and partners, in addition to in prison and "re-education" camps.

It keeps an eye on who tries to make being "part of the team" much more appealing than the outdoors. Along with wearing down the target's resistance, it is essential to give a relatively much more attractive option to what the victim is familiar from before getting the brainwasher. This can be done via a selection of techniques:

- Enabling call just with others that have currently been brainwashed. This develops a kind of peer stress that encourages the brand-new sufferer to wish like and be acknowledged by the new gathering. This might be enhanced via touch, rap sessions, group sex, or stricter methods such as a uniform dress code, managed diet regimen, or various other rigid rules.
- Rep of the message via means varying from singing or chanting the same expressions over and over, usually stressing particular keywords or phrases.
- Imitating the human heartbeat rhythm through the idea leader's speech cadence or musical accompaniment. This can be increased with lighting that's not as well dim or also extreme and an area temperature level to urge relaxation.
- Never letting the target have time to think. This can suggest just never making the target have time alone, or it can mean pounding the sufferer with repeated lectures on topics beyond comprehension while preventing inquiries.
- They provide an "us vs. them" mentality where the thought leader is right, and the outdoors is wrong. The objective is to accomplish blind obedience, to where the victim will undoubtedly commit his/her money and also life to the brainwasher and even his/her specified goals.

Acknowledge that brainwashers frequently offer benefits when the victim has actually "changed." As soon as the sufferer is broken and subordinate, they can then be reprogrammed. This can take anywhere from a few weeks to years, relying on Brainwashing situations.

- A severe kind of this complacency is known as the Stockholm syndrome, where two financial institution robbers in Sweden in 1973 held four hostages for 131 hrs. After the they were rescued, they found themselves relating to their captors, to the point that the ladies became involved with one of them, and another established a legal protection fund for the offenders.

CHAPTER 14:

HOW TO APPLY DARK PSYCHOLOGY PRACTICES IN YOUR OWN LIFE

Narcissists-- genuinely narcissistic People (conference clinical medical diagnosis) have an inflated feeling of self-worth. They require others to validate their belief in exceeding. They have imagined being worshipped as well as loved. They use dark psychology methods, influence, as well as dishonest persuasion .

Lunatics-- sociopathic Individuals (meeting professional medical diagnosis) are often attractive, smart, yet spontaneous. As a result of a lack of emotions and the ability to feel remorse, they use dark strategies to develop a surface connection and, after that, benefit from people.

Attorneys-- Some attorneys concentrate so intently on winning their request that they consider using dark persuasion strategies to obtain the result they want.

Politicians-- Some politicians use dark psychological techniques and obscure persuasion methods to convince people they are right and get votes.

Sales People-- Many salespeople ended up being so focused on achieving a sale that they utilize dark techniques to motivate and persuade a person to buy their product.

Leaders-- Some leaders use dark strategies to obtain agreement, more significant initiative, or higher efficiency from their subordinates.

Public Speakers-- Some audio speakers make use of dark techniques to enhance the emotion of the target market understanding it brings about offering more items at the back of the room.

Yes, I know. I possibly stepped on some toes. I fall under this category too.

When I'm promoting training programs on inspiration to business leaders, I am frequently asked about where the line between dark psychological methods and moral impact and persuasion methods stands? Several of these people fully admit that they commonly use these techniques or that their companies need them to make use of shady practices as a part of the firm's procedures to get and maintain clients.

This is unfortunate, as well as, although causing temporary sales and income, will eventually cause questions, poor service techniques, inadequate staff member commitment, and lasting much less effective organization results.

To better understand the difference, it's essential to assess your intent. We must ask ourselves if the tactics we are making use of help other individuals? It is okay for the consideration to be to aid you too, but if it's entirely for your benefit, you can easily fall under shady and dishonest practices.

Having an equally beneficial or a "win-win" result should be the objective. Nonetheless, you should be sincere with yourself and your idea that the other individual will profit. An instance of this is a sales representative who thinks everyone will undoubtedly take advantage of his product, and life will be much good for the clients. A sales representative with this attitude can conveniently use dark methods to relocate the person to buy and utilize an "ends justifies the methods" way of thinking.

We can ask ourself the following questions to analyze our purpose in addition to our motivation as well as persuasion methods:

- What is my objective for this interaction? The benefits and exactly how?
- Do I feel excellent regarding exactly how I am coming close to the interaction?
- Am I being entirely open and also straightforward?
- Will the result of this interaction bring about a lasting benefit for the various other individuals?
- Will the techniques I make use of lead to a more trusting partnership with the other person?

Do you wish to be successful in your management, partnerships, parenting, work, and other life locations? Then consider to establish your strategies for motivation as well as persuasion. Doing it in the correct way causes lasting credibility and influence. Doing it incorrectly (going dark) results in inadequate character, busted partnerships, and long-term failure since people at some point see through the darkness and realize your intent.

In the following list, I will review the different dark psychology and control tactics most used. This will certainly assist you to know them and prevent being controlled.

- Love Flooding
- Love Denial
- Forceful Support
- Fatigue Temptation
- Subliminal Impact
- Option Constraint
- Reverse Psychology
- Mind Games
- Indoctrination

CHAPTER 15:

DEALING WITH AN ABUSIVE OR MANIPULATIVE PARTNER

Comprehending manipulation in a partnership

Suppose your partner appeals to your instabilities or makes you feel guilty to get his/her very own way taking over control. It can show up in different types, including passive-aggressiveness, mockery as well as unjust teasing. Every case is various, and also adjustment is not always easy to pinpoint.

" If it was quickly recognizable it may not be considered manipulation," says Ikka. "If you think you are being manipulated most likely it's happening, since you find yourself doing things unlike your instinct at the prodding of somebody else's dreams or requests." Take a step back from the circumstance to determine whether the means you're feeling is an outcome of your partner's efforts to control you.

Be objective: Identify the indicators of a manipulative partnership.

To identify signs of manipulation in your connection, it's essential to take a look at your companion's practices with valuable eyes. " One of the most tough element of manipulation is recognizing it. To do so there is the need of neutrality, self-awareness, guts as well as being conscious of the patterns and practices," clarifies Ikka. Be straightforward with yourself and consider your partner's behavior without rose-colored glasses on. Talk on your own via your sensations and ask yourself what you would believe if a pal described the same situation in his or her relationship.

Approach your companion with a strategy

To note out whether you can solve the problem, you have to raise your feelings to your partner. Before you do that, carefully think of how you wish to approach the situation. Be aware that your partner might reply to your sensations by acting angered or injured, thus attracting unsecured. " Confronting a manipulator runs the risk of being more controlled, depending upon their degree of ability as well as the self-awareness of the person being manipulated," states Ikka.

Continue to maintain an impartial perspective and don't accuse your partner. Highlight what you are feeling instead of speaking directly regarding your companion's actions. " Before approaching your companion, make a list of the ways you feel you are being controlled using 'I' declarations, to ensure that you can supply concrete instances," suggests Ikka. If you stay away from any type of vital language, your companion will be most likely to respond favorably, and also the conversation will be much more constructive.

Be open to your partner's opinion.

Exactly how your companion manages your feelings will give you an idea of whether the problem can be fixed. Allow him to reply. Besides, he may not be conscious that he is acting this way. "Manipulation features an unfavorable undertone, however it's not always a resource of wickedness," says Ikka. "If the manipulator is not willingly having that behavior then the resolution comes down to efficient communication. If they're, an exit technique might be essential," she recommends.

If your companion comes to be protective and mad, or is otherwise insensitive to your sensations, consider your actions carefully. Ask yourself if you intend to be in connection with somebody who manages your feelings in this manner. It depends on you to determine if you and your companion can work together to break the manipulative practices. What's crucial is that you identify your partner's attempt to manipulate you.

" As soon as a person recognizes that they are being adjusted, exactly how they choose to handle it will certainly differ," says Ikka. "Having the ability to determine indicators of adjustment in a partnership is the secret to either getting out of one that isn't most likely to function, or managing it. It's the trickiest component."

Why people adjust

People can be manipulative because of their very own woundedness, discomfort, or immaturity. They tend to respond anxiously as opposed to easily relate. They lack the essential relational skills required for healthy communications. They either never seek or have refused self-awareness, humility, compassion, and a desire to take responsibility for their activities. Controlling is the only way they recognize on how to relate to others.

After that, some rely upon others to take care of things, pay, or cover for them, so they don't need to be accountable. Along those lines, some individuals have a personality problem and have pleasure in controlling others - even to harm them.

Manipulative individuals might have various reasons behind their activities. However, they usually fall under three major groups or styles.

Master. He or she act like the one in charge, and it's your work to do what they want without questioning - since, they say, It's for your very own wellness. They often tend to be aggressive and also easily outraged. They're bullies. Force is their primary tactic - however, they could additionally sweet-talk you into submission with magnificent beauty.

Savior (enabler, rescuer, messiah). He or she has pleased you and believes that, because they "protect" you (from whatever), you owe them a financial obligation of thankfulness for life and are anticipated to do points their means. To make you feel ashamed and bend to their will, they usually use remarks complied with reminders of things they have done for you. And like the master, the savior individuality may likewise leverage the phrase. It's for your very own excellent.

Sufferer. This person is frequently overlooked as manipulative because they're the inadequate individuals. Victims know that there's a great deal of power in appearing helpless.

No matter the manipulator's style, their pattern is the same: They regulate the action you're supposed to take, and you're intended to do what they want without pushing back. If you discover that pattern in any of your interactions, you might be in an unhealthy connection with a manipulative individual.

CHAPTER 16:

SIMPLE STRATEGIES TO READ
BODY LANGUAGE EASILY

Whether at the office or out with close friends, individuals' body language speaks. It has been studied that body language constitutes more than 60% of what we say; so, discovering to read the nonverbal signals others send out is an important ability. From eye habits to the instructions in which a person directs his/her feet, body language discloses what an individual is believing. Below are beneficial pointers to help you learn how to check out body movement and much better understand individuals you interact with.

Study the Eyes

Eye habits can be extremely telling. When connecting with someone, pay attention to whether they make straight eye contact or look away. Inability to make direct eye call can show boredom, disinterest, or perhaps deceit. If a person looks down, it typically suggests anxiety or submissiveness. Also, look for dilated pupils to figure out if someone is reacting positively toward you. Pupils expand when cognitive initiative rises, so if a person is focused on a person or something they like, their pupils will automatically dilate. Pupil dilation can be challenging to detect, but under the appropriate problems, you should have the ability to spot it. A person's blinking rate can also talk about quantities concerning what is going on inside, blinking price increases when people are interested or stressed.

Eying something can suggest a desire for that point. As an example, if someone eyes the door, this may show a need to leave. Eying an individual can indicate a need to speak with him or her. When it comes to eye habits, it is also suggested that looking upwards and to the right throughout conversation suggests a lie has been told while looking upwards and also to the left indicates the individual is telling the truth. The reason for this is that people look to the right when utilizing their creativity to make up a story and look to the left when they remember a real memory.

Gaze at the Face-- Body Movement Touching Mouth or Grinning

Although people are more likely to manage their facial expressions, you can still detect essential nonverbal signs if you pay attention. Pay particular focus to the mouth when attempting to decode nonverbal actions. A natural smile can be an active motion. Grinning is a vital nonverbal signal to watch for. There are various sorts of smiles, including real laughs as well as fake smiles. A genuine smile involves the entire face, whereas a phony smile just makes use of the mouth. A real smile suggests that the individual is happy and values the people around them. On the other hand, a phony smile is indicated to communicate satisfaction or approval but recommends that the smiler is feeling something else. A "half-smile" is an additional typical facial action that only engages one side of the mouth and indicates sarcasm or unpredictability. You might likewise notice a slight grimace that lasts less than a second before a person smile.

Take note of closeness.

Pay attention to just how close a person stands or sits alongside you to figure out if they see you favorably. Standing or being close to somebody is perhaps among the most useful indicators of connection. On the other hand, if someone supports or moves away when you move in closer, this could indicate that the link is not mutual.

See if the various other individual is matching you.

Mirroring entails resembling the various other individual's body language. When communicating with someone, check to see if the person mirrors your behavior. For example, if you are resting at a table with someone and relaxing an elbow joint on the table, wait approximately 10 seconds to see if the various other person does the same. Another typical matching gesture involve taking a sip of a drink at the same time. If somebody mimics your body movement, this is an excellent indication that she or he is attempting to establish a relationship with you. Try transforming your body posture and see if the various other person changes theirs similarly.

Observe the head activity

The rate at which a person nods their head when you are talking suggests their perseverance - or lack of. Slow responding shows that the individual is interested in what you are stating and desires you to continue talking. Quick nodding indicates the person has heard sufficient and wants you to end up talking or offer him or her a turn to speak. Turning the head sidewards during the discussion can indicate interest in what the other person is claiming. Turning the head backward can be an indicator of suspicion or uncertainty. Individuals point with the head or face at people they are interested in or share an affinity with. In teams and conferences, you can clearly see who the people with power are based on how often people look at them. On the other hand, the less-significant individuals are checked out much less frequently.

Look at the other individual's feet.

A part of our body where people usually "leak" crucial nonverbal signs is the feet. The factor people inadvertently connect nonverbal messages through their feet is since they are typically so focused on managing their faces and also top body positioning that crucial clues are revealed utilizing the feet. When standing or resting, a person will usually direct their feet in the direction they intend to go. So, if you notice that a person's feet are addressed in your instructions, this can be a good sign that they have a popular viewpoint. This applies to individual communication as well as team communication. You can inform a lot regarding group dynamics by merely studying people's body movements, precisely where their feet are pointing.

Expect hand signals

Like the feet, the hands leak vital nonverbal signs when looking at body language. This is a crucial suggestion when reading body language, so pay close attention to this next component. Seek specific hand signals, such as the other individual putting their hands in their pockets or hand on head. This can show anything from anxiety to straight-out deception. Subconscious pointing indicated by hand motions can also speak. When making hand motions, a person will direct in the individual's general instructions they share an affinity with (these nonverbal signs are particularly essential to look for during meetings, and when engaging in groups). Supporting the head with the hand by relaxing a joint on the table can suggest that the person is paying attention and is holding the head still to focus. Sustaining the head with both joints on the table, on the other hand, can show dullness.

Analyze the setting of the arms

If an individual crosses his arms while interacting with you, it is typically seen as a defensive, blocking motion. It can also suggest anxiousness, susceptibility, or a closed mind. If crossed arms are accompanied by an authentic smile as well as a total relaxed position, after that, it can suggest a positive, loosened up mindset. When somebody positions their hands on their hips, it is commonly utilized to put in importance and is used by guys more frequently than ladies.

CHAPTER 17:

7 EASY STEPS TO TAKE CONTROL OF YOUR LIFE + 5 PRACTICES YOU CAN START APPLY RIGHT NOW

Do something that scares you a little

All frequently, fear holds us back from doing what we really wish to do. When you develop the routine of encountering your concerns, you become accustomed to fear.

Sleep on a routine timetable

Obtain 7-8 hrs. of sleep a night. Go to sleep and wake up at the same time every day. The exact time isn't vital, but the range of sleep it is - you could rest from 10-- 5, or 12-- 8, or perhaps 3-- 10. It is essential to keep a routine timetable so your mind can preserve a healthy and balanced body clock. This regularity, in turn, makes it simpler to give structure and order to your life.

Save your money

When you have some money saved up, a couple of great points take place. You can occasionally manage to treat yourself to something great without worrying about the cost. A large part of your life anxiety vanishes. But possibly, most notably, when you live under your ways, you no longer need to make life choices to optimize your income - you can choose to focus on other things, like work-life balance, or following your interests.

Nevertheless, do not attempt to save money by cutting out a mug of coffee every day, or buying avocado. The simplest, most efficient method to save money is establishing an interest-bearing account and creating an automatic transfer from your account to that savings one. You won't also observe the cash going when you do not see it in the first place.

Cut down on high levels of caffeine as well as alcohol.

They both have their uses - alcohol for relaxing and socializing, caffeine for staying alert in the early mornings. But most individuals that drink them, consume way too much of them. Attempt reducing your usage by half - probably, you'll get all the same benefits, if not even more. Even better, you'll totally quit depending on caffeine and alcohol to feel good.

Please, don't own

Leasing has several benefits over owning. You understand precisely what your regular monthly price is- you're not on the hook for unforeseen fixing and maintenance prices. You're complimentary to carry on much shorter notification than a homeowner. You can also expand your financial investments, instead of having one possession that equals 500% of your net worth.

Quit spending time on social media

The social network is by far the number one way with which people waste time when they ought to be doing another thing. Worse, it usually isn't even enjoyable- social media has come to be a cesspit of pointless disagreements, unhealthy social contrast, as well as meticulous image management.

Create a side income

Having a second revenue gives the same benefits as saving money: much less stress and anxiety, more financial flexibility. But it goes better: with a side income, there's no limit to how much you can make, and if well-organized you can spend more time on it and also scale it up.

Five Practices you can start apply right now (Examples of Positive Psychology Interventions)

Substantial actions do not necessarily need to be considerable modifications in your way of living. There are many "little ideas" that can transform your practice: start re-wiring your mind for better wellness.

Gratitude Journal

It's most likely one of the most widely known positive psychology interventions. The globe's leading expert on appreciation, Robert Emmons, defines thankfulness as:

"Gratitude is a great buffer against negative emotions such as envy, hostility, concern, and irritation. It involves concentrating on the here and now moment and appreciating what it is now rather than focus on what could be". Regularly grateful individuals are:

- Healthier;
- Extra energetic;
- Extra enthusiastic;
- Experience much more frequent positive emotions.

If you enjoy writing, keeping a gratitude journal is a great means to practice gratitude. Select a time of the day when you can mirror and relax for a while and contemplate the 3 to 5 things which you are grateful for, no matter exactly how little or large they are.

To customize, you can adjust:

- The frequency;
- The layout (you could simply pick to think as opposed to writing).
- Or the several things to focus on (just one rather than three).
- Some people will undoubtedly discover an unthankful idea and replace it with a grateful one. Make this routine benefit you and suit your lifestyle.

The Thankfulness Check out.

Scientists have located that the thankfulness technique may be particularly efficient when revealed directly to one more individual.

If there's someone who had a considerable influence in your life, someone who went out of their method to assist or support you, or somebody you feel thankful because you have them in your life, write a letter of love, gratitude, and thanks that person. State carefully what he or she did and also express your appreciation in concrete terms. Then, ideally, arrange to ensure that you can speak out loud the letter to that person, either on a big day or a normal one.

In a study the gratefulness exercise participants experienced the most significant impacts and reported sensation better and less depressed, also one month after the review. An additional study by Sonja Lyubomirsky's research laboratory discovered that merely creating the gratefulness letter and not sending out or reading it to the other person still generated significant increases in happiness.

We encourage you to try it out on your own, including your spin to it. After, reflect on.

- The impact the workout had;
- How it felt when you were doing it;
- How you felt after the workout and how long it lasted;
- How are you going to continue your grateful practice?

Finest Feasible Self.

Laura King, the teacher at the College of Missouri, Columbia, designed an organized, positive outlook intervention.

Every day participants were asked to invest twenty mins writing a narrative description of their "ideal possible future selves." They were asked to ponder the most effective possible future for all the different areas of their lives.

Laura King located the participants who wrote about their visions for twenty minutes, four days in a row:

- Had quick boosts in a favorable state of mind.
- Were happier numerous weeks later on;
- They reported being sick much less commonly than individuals that were asked to write about other topics.

Consider your most important objectives in your life's different locations: professional, social, enchanting, physical, or any other classification of your choice.

Then picture your life after everything has gone as well as it perhaps can:

- What would you be doing?
- Where would you certainly be living?
- Just how would indeed your days resemble?
- Just how would certainly you feel?

This exercise can aid you to see your understanding of what self-actualization might indicate in your case.

Daily Strength Recognition.

Character Strengths and also merits are a cutting-edge category of commonly valued positive characteristics. The author's Martin Seligman and Chris Peterson examined all the significant religions and thoughtful customs to discover that the very same six virtues were valued across all cultures. These merits (humankind, courage, wisdom, etc.) needed to be based on clinical study, so they focused their research on the personality strengths that lead to them.

Positive psychology makes use of several devices to help people and organizations determine their strengths and also utilize them to boost and keep their degrees of well-being. The development of toughness needs a procedure of self-examination, self-discovery, and representation. For a person to truly understand what his/her strengths are, they need to look inward. This tool is a beneficial way to enhance self-awareness.

Use the table listed below to the checklist.

- A quick summary of the task;
- What you experienced during the activity.
- How much you delighted in the task;
- The quantity of power the activity has given;
- The possible strength or stamina being utilized.

BONUS CHAPTER:

HOW TO ANALYZE BODY LANGUAGE (DEEPENING)

When we talk about body language, we talk about the inconspicuous nonverbal signals we send and get to one another. Numerous individuals need to realize how to examine body language.

To begin with, body language can be separated into a couple of various channels:

Outward appearances: Researcher Dr Paul Ekman found seven widespread micro-expressions, or small facial motions, each human make when feeling an extraordinary emotion. We are attracted to taking a gander at and watching the face to comprehend somebody's shrouded feelings. They are an essential piece of body language.

Body Proxemics: Proxemics is a term for how our body moves in space. We are talking about how somebody is moving — would they say they are signalling? Inclining? Moving towards or away from us? Body movements reveal to us a ton about inclinations and anxiety. They are instrumental body language signals.

Decorations: Clothes, gems, shades, haircuts, are, for the most part, augmentations of our body language. Not only do certain hues and styles send signs to other people, but also how we associate with our trimmings. It is safe to say that someone is a fidgeter with their watch or ring? Do they continually self-dress or touch their hair? These are all body language signals.

Body language Principles

There are different sides to perusing body language in others. Disentangling is your capacity to examine individuals' prompts; it is how you decipher shrouded feelings, data, and personality from somebody's nonverbal. Encoding is your capacity to send prompts to others. This is the way you control your marking, what initial introduction you give, and how individuals feel when they are with you. We all know somebody with a personality that is attractive; somebody who strolls into a room and people look at him/her; somebody who talks and others tune in; somebody who was destined to lead. Or perhaps that somebody is you? Alphas have an unmistakable arrangement of nonverbal practices that mean to others in the gathering and the outside world that they are the big enchilada.

Body language That Demonstrates Attraction

To comprehend current body language signs, it is useful to have a look at the history of where it originates from. Our mountain man progenitors utilized a body language similar to the one we use today. Here are the messages we are attempting to send with our body language to potential mates, and what is viewed as appealing. Have you ever thought about how to be increasingly alluring? Fascination isn't just about looks.

Body language and Kinesics

Kinesics is the examination and understanding of nonverbal correspondence identified with the development of any piece of the body, or the body in general; in layman's terms, it is the investigation of body language. Nonetheless, Ray Birdwhistell, who is viewed as the author of this region of study, never utilized the term body language, and actually didn't think of it as suitable. He contended that what can be passed on with the body doesn't meet the etymologist's meaning of a word. Birdwhistell brought up that "human signals vary from those of different creatures in that they are polysemic, that they can be deciphered to have a wide range of implications relying upon the informative setting where they are delivered." What's more, he "opposed that 'body language' could be deciphered in some inclusive design." He likewise showed that "each body development must be deciphered extensively and related to each other component in correspondence." Regardless of that, body language is still more broadly utilized than kinesics.

Our body language is the non-verbal way we speak with the outside world – and the more significant part of us don't understand we are doing it! Body language phenomenally affects the centre of who you are as an individual; it impacts our posture and physiological wellbeing, yet it can likewise change our psychological viewpoint, our impression of the world and others' perception of us.

How our body imparts

We utilize our body language to communicate our musings, thoughts, feelings; we synchronize body movements to the words that we express. We impart purposefully through activities like shrugging our shoulders or applauding just as through inadvertent correspondence like twisting in on ourselves or guiding our feet an alternate way toward the individual we are discussing with. Before spoken language was developed, our body language was the primary technique for correspondence. Our body is our major method to speak with life!

How can it influence our state of mind?

Our body language is the way that we interface with our outside world, yet it is likewise a way that we associate with ourselves. How would you treat yourself? Do you slouch over when you walk, or do you walk tall and satisfied? It is true to say that you are thankful for each gesture your body makes for you?

Most likely not; we regularly underestimate our body; we frequently decide to condemn it. Body language can impact our physical body and posture. However, it can likewise change how we are feeling. Having a great attitude can affect misery and causes us to keep up more elevated levels of confidence and energy when we are confronted with pressure.

An up-and-coming field of psychology, known as installed comprehension, asserts that the association between our body and our general surroundings doesn't merely impact us. However, we are personally woven into the way that we think. Studies in this field show that the individuals who are sitting in a hard seat are less inclined to bargain than those sitting in a delicate chair, and those holding warm beverages saw others as more mindful and liberal than those having cold drinks. This examination shows that body language is a two-way road prompting both the outside and inward world.

Four different ways you can change your body language

The followings are four ways you can change your body language.

Flip around that glare!

Smiling is infectious! A complete report on smiling found that it can enact the cerebrum examples of positive feelings. So, smile, and do it frequently! Regardless of whether you are having an awful day, smile at any rate! It may very well assist you with turning the day around!

Crossing your arms

Crossing the arms is a resistance system to ensure the heart and lungs. We regularly do it when we feel shaky, anxious, or disturbed. The physical obstruction gives others the feeling that we are cut off and detached from them.

This gesture by and broad idea is thought to be an aggressive body posture, anyway a few investigations have indicated that crossing the arms can cause individuals progressively industrious when they feel like stopping.

Force presenting

One of the significant specialists in the zone of body language is Amy Cuddy. In her TedTalk, she talks about how body language can be the contrast among succeeding and coming up short at prospective employee meet-ups. She made members remain in high force stances and low force models for two minutes before sending them into a top weight talk with the employer. She estimated levels of the pressure hormone cortisol and the predominance hormone testosterone. The outcomes demonstrated that those remaining in high force presence had expanded degrees of testosterone and lower levels of cortisol than those in little force presence.

Quit slumping

This may appear obviously evident; however, slumping not just influences your spine, it can likewise change your state of mind! Indeed, slumping can prompt back agony and an irregular spine arrangement. Intellectually, it can leave you feeling miserable, lacking vitality, and shut off from others. Sitting and standing up straighter can assist with settling back torment just as lift your life and state of mind.

Changing your posture can be difficult for your body from the outset, particularly on the off chance that you are accustomed to slumping over for significant periods! You may feel muscle hurts in the neck, back, and bears – don't stress, this will pass!

Improve your posture in order to improve your temperament!

Body language isn't likely the first sport you'd think to look when you are experiencing a low state of mind, however, investigating our body language can reveal to us how we are truly feeling. Our body language has an immediate connection to our temperament, similarly to our mindset that has some influences to our posture.

Simple ways you can fix your posture to adjust your state of mind:

- Smile when you are having a terrible day!
- Unfold your arms when you feel anxious and allow yourself to be available to circumstances
- Turning the palms of your hands forward when you walk will urge the shoulders to unwind back as opposed to moving advances
- Power present before pressure instigating situations such as prospective employee meet-ups

Body language signs when someone hides something from you

Untrustworthiness. It can happen in many connections — and a great deal of the time, it accomplishes more mischief than anything. It's once in a while ever astute to keep insider facts from your accomplice in a relationship. You never need to keep your accomplice in obscurity about a lot of things in your lives together. It shows that you don't regard your accomplice enough to recognize that they are deserving of reality. You are saying that they aren't sufficient to be determined what's genuine – and that is, in every case, terrible in a relationship. You generally need to confess all to your accomplice, especially about vital issues encompassing your relationship.

Be that as it may, a big deal of us are childish. Here and there, reality can be difficult to stomach. Every now and then, a fact can place us in an extreme condition of a burden once it's uncovered. So a great deal of us will turn to lie just to spare our butts. Your man may be blameworthy of doing as such. He may be keeping you out of the loop about something that he should be opening up to you about.

What's more, that is hazardous for a relationship. You can't hope to make your link work appropriately in case you're not being taken care of the entirety of the best possible realities. You generally need to ensure that you know everything that is going on, so you don't wind up getting either tricked or bushwhacked by anything.

Men aren't generally the best verbal communicators. You may likely know this at this point. Be that as it may, he does consistently tend to communicate through his body language and his physical developments. His intuitive may disclosed to you a lot of things about himself without him in any event, seeing it. You simply need to willingly volunteer to ensure that you spot out the signs when they present themselves. You need to ensure that you keep steady over things in your relationship. Here are some essential body language signs that your man is concealing something from you.

1. HE CROSSES HIS ARMS WHEN HE TALKS TO YOU.

He may not see that he's actually doing it. He's subliminally folding his arms since he's attempting to secure something. He wouldn't like to give the whole access. He's shutting himself off to you in a specific way. He wouldn't want to provide you with full access, and that is exactly the reason he's utilizing his arms as a boundary.

2. HE DOES NOT FACE HIS BODY TOWARDS YOU WHEN YOU'RE SPEAKING.

It's conspicuous that he is attempting to conceal something if his body shifts towards another bearing when he's conversing with you. Rather than utilizing his arms as a method of safeguard, he just totally closes the entryway on you by dismissing.

3. HE DOES NOT LOOK STRAIGHT INTO YOUR EYES DURING CONVERSATIONS.

He doesn't need you to see the dread in his eyes. He doesn't require you to see reality by looking deep into his spirit. The eyes are the windows to the soul.

4. HE SEEMS EASILY IRRITABLE WHENEVER YOU ASK HIM QUESTIONS.

He gets hugely guarded when you ask him necessary inquiries concerning his life. He is going to cause it to appear as though you're investigating him in any given event, when you're actually not. The weight is beginning to get to him, and he's going to wind up acting too fractious. He wouldn't like to get trapped in his falsehoods.

5. HE ACTS ALL FIDGETY WHENEVER IT'S JUST THE TWO OF YOU.

He is eager. The mystery is genuinely squeezing him. There's such a significant amount of vitality within him that he needs to discharge in one way or another. He needs to diminish the entirety of that pressure. That is the reason he will experience issues keeping still.

6. HE TRIES TO MAINTAIN A VERY STRICT EXPRESSION ON HIS FACE ALL THE TIME.

He has a poker face on. Additionally, he's undoubtedly attempting to shroud something – much like in poker. He doesn't need you to recognize what cards he's holding. He's keeping his cards hidden from everyone else, and he's definitely under a great deal of pressure.

7. HE ACTS LIKE A BLINKING MACHINE.

Brain research has demonstrated that individuals who are lying or who are keeping mysteries will, in general, flicker at a quick rate. So be very careful about the recurrence of his flickering.

8. HE BITES HIS FINGERNAILS.

Brain research has additionally expressed that the demonstration of gnawing fingernails is an indication of either uncertainty or nervousness. On the off chance that he's restless about the mystery he's stowing away, he will be chewing his fingernails frequently.

9. HE LASHES OUT AT YOU A LOT.

He is so blameworthy about the mystery that he's stowing away. He realizes that it's inappropriate to keep something from you. The blame is beginning to gobble him up inside. Furthermore, he's attempting to carry on because of that blame. He will reverse the situation on you and cause it to appear as though you're the person who is accomplishing something incorrectly.

Getting and Understanding Nonverbal Signals

Lauren murmured. She'd quite recently gotten an email from her chief, Gus, saying that the item proposition she'd been taking a shot at would not have been closed down all things considered. It didn't bode well. Seven days prior, she'd been in a gathering with Gus, and he'd appeared to be extremely positive about everything. Of course, he hadn't looked, and he continued watching out of the window at something. In any case, she'd recently put that down to him being occupied. Furthermore, he'd said that "the task will most likely stretch the go-beyond."

On the off chance that Lauren had discovered somewhat progressively about body language, she'd have understood that Gus was attempting to reveal to her that he wasn't "sold" on her thought. He simply wasn't utilizing words.

Tricks to Read Negative Body Language

Monitoring negative body language in others allows you to get on implicit issues or awful emotions. Along these lines, in this area, we'll feature some negative nonverbal signs that you should pay some attention to.

Troublesome Conversations and Defensiveness

Troublesome or tense discussions are an awkward unavoidable truth grinding away. Maybe you've needed to manage an annoying client, or expected to have a conversation with somebody about their terrible showing. Or then again, perhaps, you've arranged a significant agreement.

In a perfect world, these circumstances would be settled tranquillity. Be that as it may, regularly, they are entangled by sentiments of apprehension, stress, preventiveness, or even resentment. However, we may attempt to shroud them; these feelings regularly appear through in our body language. For instance, on the chance that somebody is showing at least one of the accompanying practices, he will most likely be withdrawn, uninvolved, or miserable:

- Arms collapsed before the body.
- Insignificant or tense outward appearance.
- The body got some distance from you.
- Eyes depressed, keeping in touch.
- Keeping away from Unengaged Audiences

At the point when you have to convey an introduction or to work together in a gathering, you need the individuals around you to be 100% locked in. Here are some "obvious" signs that individuals might be exhausted or unbiased in what you're stating:

- I am sitting drooped, looking sad.
- Looking at something different, or into space.
- Squirming, picking at garments, or tinkering with pens and telephones.
- Composing or doodling.

Tricks to read Positive Body Language

At the point when you utilize positive body language, it can add solidarity to the verbal messages or thoughts that you need to pass on, and help you to abstain from imparting blended or befuddling signs. In this segment, we'll portray some fundamental postures that you can embrace in order to extend fearlessness as well as receptiveness.

Establishing a Confident First Connection

These tips can assist you in adjusting your body language, so you establish a special first connection:

Have an open posture. Be loose; however, don't slump! Sit or stand upstanding and place your hands by your sides. Make sure you abstain from remaining with your hands on your hips, as this will cause you to seem more significant, which can convey animosity or craving to rule.

Utilize a firm handshake. However, don't become overly energetic! You certainly don't need to get unbalanced or, more regrettable, excruciating for the other individual. On the off chance that it does, you'll likely seem to be impolite or forceful.

Keep in touch. Try to maintain eye contact with the other person for a couple of moments one after another. This will give her that you're right as well as locked in. Be that as it may, abstain from transforming it into a gazing match!

Abstain from contacting your face. There's a typical discernment that individuals who get their appearances while addressing questions are being untrustworthy. While this isn't in every case valid, it's ideal to abstain from tinkering with your hair or contacting your mouth or nose, especially if your point is to seem to be reliable.

Public Speaking

Positive body language can likewise assist you with engaging individuals, to veil introduction nerves, and in order to extend certainty whenever you talk in public. Here are many tips that can help you in doing this:

Have a positive posture. Sit or stand upstanding, with your shoulders back and your arms unfurled and at your sides or before you. Try not to be enticed to place your hands in your pockets, or to slump, as this will make you look unbiased.

Keep your head up. Your head should be upstanding and level. Inclining excessively far advance or in reverse can make you look forceful or self-important.

Practice and improve your posture. You'd practice your introduction in advance, so why not practice your body language, as well? Remain casually, with your weight equally balanced. Keep one foot somewhat before the other – this will assist you with maintaining your posture.

Utilize free hand motions. Spread your hands separated, before you, with your palms confronting marginally toward your crowd. This demonstrates an ability to convey and to share thoughts. Keep your upper arms next to your body. Maintain a strategic distance from over-expression, or individuals may give more consideration to your hands than to what you're stating.

9 Secrets to Read People

The capacity to peruse others will extraordinarily influence how you manage them. With that being said, what would it be advisable for you to tune in for? What's more, what different signs can warn you to what somebody is thinking or feeling? "You shouldn't be a first-rate investigator to make sense of what is happening in somebody's mind. The signs are consistently there- - you should simply recognize what to search for." Here are nine hints in order to be able to read others:

1. Make a benchmark

People have various quirks and examples of conduct. For instance, they may make a sound as if to speak, take a gander at the floor while talking, fold their arms, scratch head, stroke their neck, squint, mope, or shake their feet the majority of the time.

People show these practices for various reasons. They could mostly be idiosyncrasies. Some of the time, nonetheless, these similar activities could be characteristic of misleading, outrage, or even apprehension. Making a psychological gauge of others' ordinary conduct will surely help you.

2. Search for deviations

Focus on irregularities between the gauge you've made and the individual's words and emotions. For instance: you've seen that a significant provider of yours has the propensity for making a sound as if to speak over and over when apprehensive. As he acquaints some moderately little changes with your business course of action, he begins to do this. You may choose to test further, therefore posing a couple of a more significant number of inquiries than you would regularly have.

3. Notice bunches of signals

No solitary signal or word necessarily implies anything; however, when a few social deviations are bunched together, pay heed. For example, not exclusively does your provider continues to make a sound as if to speak. Nevertheless, he likewise does that head-scratching thing. Additionally, he keeps rearranging his feet. Continue with alert.

4. Investigate

Alright, so you've seen that a person is acting somewhat not the same as expected. Move your perception up an indent to check whether and when that individual rehashes similar conduct with others in your gathering. Keep on observing the individual as the person associates with others in the room. Does personal demeanour change? What about their stance and non-verbal communication?

5. Investigate the mirror

Mirror neurons are worked in screens in our cerebrum that reflect others' perspectives. We are wired to peruse each other's non-verbal communication. A grin initiates the grin muscles in our countenances, while a glare actuates our grimace muscles. At the point when we see somebody we like, our eyebrows curve, facial muscles unwind, head tilts, and blood streams to our lips, making them full. If your accomplice doesn't respond that conduct, this individual could be sending you a consistent message: he or she doesn't care for you or aren't content with something you might have done.

6. Distinguish the reliable voice

The most remarkable individual isn't generally the one sitting at the leader of the table. Sure, people have reliable voices. Around a meeting room table, the most certain individual is probably going to be the most impressive one: far-reaching stance, authentic voice as well as a significant grin. (Try not to confound a loud sound with a solid one.)

In case you're trying out a plan to a gathering, it's anything but difficult to focus on the pioneer of the group. Be that as it may, that pioneer may have an invalid character. In reality, the person in question relies vigorously upon others to decide and is virtually impacted by them. Distinguish the reliable voice, and your odds for progress increment drastically.

7. See how they walk

As a rule, people who mix along, come up short on a streaming movement in their developments or hold their head down need fearlessness. On the chance that you notice these attributes in a colleague, put forth an additional attempt to offer honour, trying to help assemble the individual's confidence. Or on the other hand, you may need to pose the person in question more straightforward inquiries during a gathering to haul those good thoughts out away from any confining influence.

8. Pinpoint activity words

As an FBI specialist, I discovered words were the closest path for me to get into someone else's head. Stories speak to contemplations, so recognize the name that is freighted with importance. For instance, if your supervisor says she's "chose to go with brand X," the activity word is chosen. This single word demonstrates that most probable your supervisor 1) isn't incautious, 2) gauged a few choices, and 3) thoroughly considers things. Activity words offer experiences into how an individual thinks.

9. Search for character pieces of information

Many of us have a remarkable character. Yet there arc fundamental explanations that can assist you with identifying with someone else so you can understand the person in the question precisely.

- Does somebody display increasingly withdrawn or outgoing conduct?
- Does the person in question appear to be driven by connections or centrality?
- How does the individual handle hazard and vulnerability?
- What takes care of their self-image?
- What are the individual's practices when pushed?
- What are the individual's practices when loose?

Furthermore, there are exceptional cases for each standard. Be that as it may, remembering these standards as you assemble your forces of perception will incredibly upgrade your capacity to understand others, comprehend their reasoning, and impart adequately as well.

Instructions to Read a Person

It's conceivable to peruse an individual if you give close consideration to their non-verbal communication, what they state, how they say it, and your instinct as well as emotions. You can never know an individual's musings without a doubt. However, you can pick up hints about their considerations and character by utilizing a couple of crucial techniques.

Method#1. Reading Body Language

1. Study act. Stance can give several insights about what an individual is honestly thinking. How they sit and how they lean recounts to a story. Somewhere in the range of 70 and 90% of correspondence can be non-verbal. If an individual incline from you, they are most likely inclined to stress.

On the off chance that they are reclining as though they are loose, it tends to be a pointer that they feel incredible and in charge. A weak stance can imply that an individual needs confidence or harbours negative emotions.

2. Recognize positive non-verbal communication. Specialists isolate non-verbal communication into positive and negative development classifications. You can distinguish whether an individual feels decidedly toward you by spotting positive non-verbal communication moves.

- Not crossing arms or legs shows positive emotions.
- Turning away, as though modest, is an indication of positive feeling towards you.
- Inclining towards you is considered to be a positive non-verbal communication development.

3. Recognize negative non-verbal communication. Specific prompts should show to you that the individual may harbour negative emotions toward you or themselves.

- Intersection arms or legs are a development that shows carefulness.
- Pointing feet away or towards a leave implies that an individual might have negative sentiments.
- Looking to the side or inclining ceaselessly is an indication of negative non-verbal communication.
- At the point when an individual touches their nose, eyes, or back of the neck, it is a sign that can show negative emotions.

4. Spot counterfeit grins. Some signs show that an individual's smile isn't veritable. In a real smile, you will see the wrinkles around an individual's eyes. In a phoney smile, you frequently won't. Grinning truly utilizes increasingly facial muscles.

- The chuckle lines or wrinkles around the eye are brought about by the orbicularis oculi and are muscles actuated in veritable grins.
- Quick grins are less inclined to be veritable.
- Counterfeit grins are, in some cases, higher due to the fact that the individual is attempting to extend their face.

5. Peruse an individual's eyes. The eyes are expressive, and it's conceivable to inform a great deal regarding an individual if you comprehend what to search for in them. Widened understudies show intrigue. Force looking methods means that an individual just investigates the triangle from your eyes to your temple, which means they are maintaining a strategic distance from closeness. On the off chance that they look from your eyes to your mouth and down, that demonstrates a craving for intimacy. Looking from the eyes to the mouth only is called social looking and shows solace and fellowship.

Supported eye to eye connection can show an endeavour to overwhelm or can part with the fact that an individual is lying. Regard to eye connection for a few seconds before turning away definitely implies confidence. Eye to eye connection for one second or less shows either avoidance or instability.

- Fast flickering can be a sign an individual is keen on you.

- Liars will frequently look to one side when thinking. A few specialists accept this is because they are creating a story.

- Shutting the eyes for a continued timeframe implies an individual needs some time to think.

6. Peruse an individual's hands. Similarly, as with the eyes, the hands can give you pieces of information about an individual's character or what they are thinking. At the point when an individual holds their palms down, it shows they feel ground-breaking. A descending palm can likewise be an indication that something is being either dismissed or halted. At the point when an individual keeps their palms up, it can show accommodation.

7. Understand signals and contact. How people use their hands can give you pieces of information about what they are thinking. Signals are characterized as physical developments that uncover feelings or assessment.

- At the point when somebody contacts your hand quickly, it shows they need an association with you.

- At the point when an individual rubs their nose, they may be lying.
- If an individual conceals their hands, they may be covering up something from you.
- At the point when an individual lays their jawline on their hand, they're settling on a choice.
- Taking care of the neck implies an individual has unanswered inquiries.
- Watch out for reflecting motions. At the point when an individual begins to duplicate your looks and signals, for the majority of times, it implies they need to sell you something.
- Moving into private space can be an indication of terrorizing.
- Causing a stir implies an individual ponders you and needs to convey better.

8. Understand the ears. Numerous people neglect the ears, yet refined face perusers accept that they can offer signs to the character.

Little ears show a meticulousness and assurance.

People with ears that stick out might be courageous sorts who are available to attempt new things.

At the point when people have ears that are high on their heads, it can demonstrate they are scholarly and significant masterminds.

Method#2. Reading Verbal Cues

1. Study word decision. Words people use can offer intimations to their conduct. For example, if an individual discloses to you, they won "another" grant, this gives some insight that they are unreliable because they needed to guarantee you realized they'd won previously. This reveals to you it is successful in offering applause for achievements. It pinpoints a zone of helplessness. Study whether an individual's assertion decision coordinates their non-verbal communication.

2. Spot lying. It's conceivable to spot whether an individual may be lying dependently on what they state. Think about their remarks in setting, however, and consistently know that reading, verbal signals isn't idiot-proof.

- Utilizing an inquiry to address an investigation gives them more opportunities to make up a story.

- At the point when people include qualifiers like "as far as I could possibly know," they may be lying.

- At the point when people are lying, they will, once in a while, expel references to themselves, maintaining a strategic distance from utilization of "I."

- When lying, people, sometime, utilize the current state to allude to past occasions.

A few investigations have discovered that people who utilize progressively formal discourse may be lying. For instance, they probably won't use compressions or will utilize titles. People who are liable for something will, every now and then, use words that mellow the demonstration. For instance, rather than a name like taking, they may utilize a comment like obtain.

3. Focus on the tone and speed of the voice. The sounds people radiate when they talk can be excessively uncovering about their characters.

- People who talk excessively quick and a lot are typically unreliable or on edge.
- Moaning shows pity and disappointment.
- On the off chance that individual talks too gradually, they might be discouraged or need immediacy.
- On the off chance that an individual's voice changes pitch out of nowhere, they may be lying.
- A dreary manner of speaking demonstrates unscrupulousness.
- Men may differ their manner of speaking more when they are pulled in to a lady.

4. Understanding the length of the sentence. The average sentence contains 10 to 15 words. This is known as the "mean/average length of articulation." Longer or shorter sentences than reasonable means that pressure. A few specialists trust you can tell an individual is lying on the off chance that they veer off from the mean length of articulation fundamentally. They will single out those sentences to concentrate more intently.

Method#3. Reading Emotional Energy

1. Shake hands. When you shake an individual's hands, what's your feeling of their vitality? Give careful consideration of what you feel. Do you feel warmth or chilliness?

- Chinese medication has a word for the vitality and individual emits Chi.
- Another word for passionate vitality is an individual's "vibe."

In order to survey an individual's vitality, you may need to contact them through an embrace or handshake or just by touching their hand.

2. Utilize your instinct. Don't overthink it. Does the only cause you to feel great or not? Now and then, you simply have a "premonition" you should focus on. Goose pimples can be a physical sign the body gives you that discloses to you something isn't right. Or on the other hand, they will show a feeling of history repeating itself. Does a specific cause makes you feel depleted or stimulated? This gives you pieces of information to their passionate vibe. Focus on flashes of knowledge that intrude on your reasoning. What's your feeling of an individual's general vitality? Not a motion or tone anywhere, yet the available air they make and feeling they radiate?

3. Peruse their eyes. Passionate vitality radiates through in the eyes and look. The adage "the eyes are the window to the spirit" was made, which is as it should be. Do they look stiff and irate or delicate and inviting? Closeness can be made through a basic look. Give careful consideration to the non-verbal communication around the eyes.

4. Peruse an individual's vitality type. Old scholars created five components to depict an individual's general vitality. They thought understanding these components could assist you with reading people and even spot sickness.

- People with fire vitality are ostentatious, crazy, and energizing.
- An individual who has wood vitality is fundamental, new, and energetic.
- People with earth vitality are reasonable and precise as well.
- People with mental vitality are discouraged and pulled back.
- Water vitality is a pointer of tranquillity and objectivity.

Body language and How To Read It

At the point when we talk about non-verbal communication, we take a gander at the subtle signs we send and get to one another nonverbally. Numerous people need to realize how to peruse non-verbal communication. To begin with, non-verbal communication can be separated into a couple of various channels:

Outward appearances: Researcher Dr Paul Ekman found seven general microexpressions or small facial motions each human causes whenever they feel a painful feeling. We are attracted to take a gander at and watching the face to comprehend somebody's concealed feelings. They are an essential piece of non-verbal communication.

Body Proxemics: Proxemics is a term that defines how our body moves in space. We are continually taking a gander at how somebody is moving, would they say they are signalling? Inclining? Moving towards or away from us? Body developments disclose to us a great deal about inclinations and apprehension. They are instrumental in non-verbal communication signs.

Trimmings: Clothes, adornments, shades, haircuts, are, for the most part, augmentations of our non-verbal communication. Not exclusively do certain hues and styles impart signs to other people; how we associate with our trimmings is saying something additional. Is it true that someone is a fidgeter with their watch or ring? Do they continually self-dress or contact their hair? These are all non-verbal communication signs. There are different sides to reading non-verbal communication in others.

Translating is your capacity to peruse people's signs. It is how you decipher shrouded feelings, data, and character from somebody's non-verbal. Encoding is your capacity to send alerts to others. This is how you control your marking, the initial introduction you give and how you make people feel when they are with you.

CONCLUSIONS

Dark Psychology is the most dominant powers at work and today. It is everywhere and it is utilized by many dominant influencers the world has ever known. The individuals who ignore its existence most likely are exposed to it and who doesn't know how to use it are afraid of having it used against them. Knowing its advantages and strength will give great possibilities in your daily life, but be conscious of the ethical side of it; no matter the area in your life you would like to use it: at work, in a relationship, with your friends, manipulation could give you advantage and great result.

Be careful and mindful that no one in your environment is using it against you; learn all the trick to recognize it and to use on your favor all its trick.

DID YOU KNOW THAT CAN DOWNLOAD FOR FREE THE AUDIOBOOK VERSION OF THIS BOOK, PLUS TWO MORE?

CLICK HERE FOR AUDIBLE US

CLICK HERE FOR AUDIBLE UK

CLICK HERE FOR AUDIBLE FR

CLICK HERE FOR AUDIBLE DE